By Blood, Bone, and Blade:
A Tribute to the Morrigan
Second Edition

Edited by Nicole Bonvisuto

Copyright © 2014 by Neos Alexandrina

All rights reserved. No part of this book may be reproduced by any means or in any form whatsoever without written permission from the author(s), except for brief quotations embodied in literary articles or reviews. Copyright reverts to original authors after publication.

Cover art image (c) Ashley Bryner 2012, lindowyn.com, with thanks to Marcus Raynum, Obsidiandawn.com, and shd-stock.deviantart.com

Dedications and Thank Yous

Thank you to all the patient souls who waited for this anthology to finally emerge on paper. Thank you to the patient editors at Bibliotheca Alexandrina. Thank you to the watchful eye of my husband, helping me proof-read the final edits. Thank you to everyone who submitted their thoughts, experiences, and souls in print to be added to this devotional.

Thank you to the Phantom Queen, who sees the beginning and the end of all things. This is for you, Lady, and all those who honor you, knowing and unknowing, seeing and unseeing, until the day you call them home.

Table of Contents

Introduction: A Tribute to An Morrígan
    by Nicole Bonvisuto   xi
A Note From the EiC
    by Rebecca Buchanan   xiii

Testimonials, Poetry, and Essays

Morrigan
    by Morpheus Ravenna   1
The Morrigan Speaks
    by Stephanie Woodfield   2
Macha Speaks the Sun (Recollections from Trance)
    by Hope Maree Foley   3
Hymn I to The Morrigan
    by Valiel Elentári   5
Hymn II to The Morrigan
    by Valiel Elentári   6
Banshee
    by Ashley R. Bryner   7
Nemain ~ Queen of the Battle Frenzy
    by Vivienne Moss   9
Invocation to Nemain
    by Vivienne Moss   12
Reign
    by S. E. Acker   13
The Morrigan ~ My Queen
    by Vivienne Moss   14
Morrigan
    by Morgaine Nightshade   16
Nine Times Eternal:
    The Ongoing Transformations of the Great Queen
    by L. Sixfingers   17
Words Of The Morrigan
    by Raven Spirit   28

Morrigan Above Stonehenge
  by Morgaine Nightshade 29
A Testimonial
  by Copper Moon 30
The Morrígan and Cú Chulainn:
  A More Nuanced View of Their Relationship
  by P. Sufenas Virius Lupus 31
Call to the Morrighan
  by Frances Billinghurst 46
Macha ~ One Face of the Morrigan
  by Morgan Daimler 47
An Expansion of Babd's Prophecy
  from the Second Battle of Mag Tuired
  by Judith O'Grady 51
Fulacht na Morrígna
  by P. Sufenas Virius Lupus 52
Badb Catha
  by Stephanie Woodfield 54
An Morrigan
  by Sandy Nickell 55
The Crow's Call
  by Monika Pleyer 56
Valkyrie Queen
  by Sara Star 57
The Morrigan, Allecto, and Lamia: Irish Deities
  and Interpretatio Hibernica of Classical Myth
  by P. Sufenas Virius Lupus 58
The Washer at the Ford
  by Jennifer Lawrence 70
Letter to the Morrigan
  by Xochiquetzal Duti Odinsdottir 71
How I Met the Morrigan
  by Hannah Lipsky 74
Advice
  by Jennifer Lawrence 80
Shieldmaiden's Song
  by Morpheus Ravenna 82

Raven
    by Morgaine Nightshade   84
The Morrigan's Charge
    by Morgaine Nightshade   87
I Am
    by Morgaine Nightshade   86
The Mother's Words
    by Morgaine Nightshade   87
When The Morrigan Calls
    by Blackbird O'Connell   89
Acquiescence
    by Kim Cairelle Perilloux   91
The Morrigan
    by Adrian Barlow   93
Morrigan's Ride
    by Gebirgsjägerinne   94
Raven's Wings
    by Ophelia Anu   95
Musings on the Irish War Goddesses
    by Saigh Kym Lambert   98
Great Queen
    by Michael Routery   160
The Blood Crow
    by Gerri Leen   161
Lady Dusk, Mother of Night
    by Christa A. Bergerson   162
The Scorned Woman Conjures the Morrigan
    by Christa A. Bergerson   163
How the Morrigan Taught Me to See
    by Rebecca Buchanan   164
Morrigan in Black and White
    by Morgaine Nightshade   165
You Will Know Me
    by Jennifer Lawrence   166

Fiction in Her Honor

Bookfront
    by Nicole Bonvisuto — 171
Sometimes You Do
    by Diotima Sophia — 172
Shell Shock
    by Juli D. Revezzo — 177
Macha's Curse
    by Stephanie Woodfield — 189
Through the Gloom
    by Diotima Sophia — 192
Morrigan, Wolf-Eyed
    by Sarah Sinopa — 195
The Morrigan's Story
    by Rufus Brock Maychild — 196
New Word
    by Diotima Sophia — 199
Badb's Song
    by Stephanie Woodfield — 202
Ravens
    by Diotima Sophia — 204

Rituals, Prayers, and Recipes

The Morrighan
    by Katy de Haviland — 207
How to Build an Altar to the Morrigan
    by Rebecca Buchanan — 208
Morrigan Altar
    by Blackbird O'Connell — 209
Prayer to The Morrigan
    by Galina Krasskova — 210
Prayer to the Morrigan for Blessing
    by Morgan Daimler — 211
Invocation of Morrigu
    by Morgan Daimler — 212

Prayer to An Morrígan
    by Blackbird O'Connell   213
Prayer to The Morrigan for Protection
    by Morgan Daimler   214
Morrigan Prayer
    by Sophie Reicher   215
Song to The Morrigan
    by Morgan Daimler   216
Samhain Invocation for The Morrigan
    by Adrian Barlow   218
A Prayer to The Morrigan
    by Judith O'Grady   219
Morrigan, Warrior Queen
    by Sara Star   220
An Invocation to The Morrigan
    by Judith O'Grady   221
Reclaiming Power with The Morrigan
    by David Salisbury   222
Source of Enchantments:
    A Devotional Rite of the Mórrígan
    by L. Sixfingers   227
Morrighan's Flight
    by Alexis J. Money   235
Invocation of the Morrighan Ritual ~ Dark of the Moon
    by Shea Morgan   236
Dedication Ritual to An Morrígan
    by Blackbird O'Connell   246
Nemain Blessing Amulet
    by Sophie Reicher   250
Badb Amulet
    by Sophie Reicher   251
Morrigan Incense and Morrigan Blessing Oil
    by Galina Krasskova   252
Morrigan Incense and Morrigan Oil
    from the Iseum of the Star*Eyed Warrior   253

Our Contributors	255
About Bibliotheca Alexandrina	267
Current Titles	268
Forthcoming Titles	269

x

Introduction: A Tribute to An Morrigan

I first met The Morrigan in service to a friend. She was in a terrible situation where she feared for her safety, and asked her spiritual house to appeal to our patrons as well as hers for protection. We called to The Morrigan empty-handed and empty-headed, beseeching her protection with nothing in its place to offer. She demanded that we present a sacrifice for our request: if we valued this woman's life so much, then who would put their own on the line for it? That evening ended with the flat of a broadsword against the back of my neck as I pledged to serve Her for a year and a day.

Since then, I have faded in and out of the service of the Raven Queen for years. While I am owned by Loki, I know that She is always with me and has no issue making it known when She is in need of my direct attentions and service. For example, the final straw in knowing that this devotional was necessary was a crow diving at the windshield of my car whilst I considered the matter.

I have known Her as the loving mother in times of duress. My favorite memory of Her support involves a rather strange event when I was going in for a medical procedure I was very anxious over. At a time when Michigan's crow population had been ravaged by the West Nile Virus and any member of the Corvidae family was a rare sight, the entire yard of the doctor's office was positively packed with crows. I knew, in that moment, that everything was going to be fine.

I have known Her wrath when I directly refused her orders to leave an abusive relationship and suffered from health problems that no doctor's directions could cure.

Over my years of service, I have come to love The Morrigan. She has driven me forward in times of defeat when I felt I had nothing left to give. She has been my succor in times of great pain and hardship.

I have encountered many who love Her and many who fear Her, but very few published writings on Her modern-day honor and service.

I am most honored to be able to collect the thoughts and words of so many of her devotees and followers. For those serving, their words will be known. For those searching, they will have resources guide them. In any context, She will be honored.

This is for you, Lady, in all of your forms.

Hail to the Phantom Queen!

Nicole Bonvisuto
Winter 2014

A Note From the EiC

Night Hag. The Black Queen. The Raven Who Screams.

There are Gods whom I love. There are Gods who inspire me. There are Gods who drive me. There are Gods who perplex me. And there are Gods who terrify me: Dionysus. Kali. Odin. And -- yes -- The Morrigan.

As always, there are lessons to be learned in that fear. While contributing to this devotional in Her honor has not lessened my terror of The Morrigan, it has taught me to understand, channel, and even embrace that fear.

And so, the first of many thanks I offer to Her for a lesson well-taught: Iron Beak, Mistress of Battles, Phantom Queen: The Morrigan.

Rebecca Buchanan
Winter 2014

Testimonials, Poetry, and Essays

Morrigan
by Morpheus Ravenna

The Morrigan Speaks . . .
by Stephanie Woodfield

Your first and last breath belong to Me
I who am the embodiment
Of destruction and creation
Who revels in the chaos of change
It is only I who can navigate you through the ruins of your soul
So, you call me the Dark Mother,
The Raven of War
And I am, and I am not
For I am ever and only Myself
Beyond the definitions of humanity
If I destroy it is only to create anew
From the ashes of the old
I am the fertile darkness
Deep within the soul
I am the forge that tempers the Will
I am the rage that empowers
I am the soul that will not suffer or endure injustice
I am the strength that emerges from the darkness of self doubt
Self-knowledge attained from loss
So drink in My Darkness
And discover the beauty within
And learn the wisdom that only I can teach

"The Morrigan Speaks" originally appears on page 129 of *Celtic Lore & Spellcraft of the Dark Goddess* by Stephanie Woodfield © 2011 Llewellyn Worldwide, Ltd. 2143 Wooddale Drive, Woodbury, MN 55125.
All rights reserved, used by permission.

Macha Speaks the Sun
(Recollections from Trance)
by Hope Maree Foley

I awoke in a river of blood. Not the kind that spills from violence with the stench of rage and the flavour of fear and courage, but rather the kind that spills into your veins from the past; the river of heart-blood that pours from those who have walked before you, rich in knowing.

I heard her long before I saw her, voicing a grief the depths of which drew me to call in kind for justice and release and so I waded, compelled, driven by the current and pulled by her wailing, a sound so unearthly that it was not my ears that heard it, but the ocean in my flesh, capturing the echo like the sound of waves beating inside a seashell clasped to an ear.

When I found her, it was not my eyes that saw, but the sun inside my heart, shining fierce, relentless love upon a land, one moment baked dry with the furious heat of battle, the next flooded with tears for the fallen and lost. The blood of the river ran from her; as tears from her eyes, as life from her womb and as an endless, sinuous gift from the cloth that she wrung and rinsed, wrung and rinsed, her fingers moving with the tenderness of a mother, with the grace of a bold lover, working the shrouds of her beloved troops back to funereal white.

When her eyes met mine, the fabric of me faded and I was only the blood that washed me. I was of the river – I was of her. Time left us and my breath, suspended, held me like a surfacing bubble, infinitesimal fireworks inside of me, threatening to burst and set me adrift in ecstatic pieces, unable to hold together without the thread of my material self. Then, in that explosion, the light of the sun filled my senses and I was whole again, feet firm upon an ancient ground.

I smelled the wrenching mephitis of recently abandoned battle, sanguinary and fetid, but comforting like the surety of Death and his peace. I looked about to see earth flushed crimson with the casualties of honour, gone now to seek the next path on the wing of a raven.

She was there too, of course, this time in silence, wearing the sun for a crown with its rays tumbling down to clothe her in shimmering gold and suddenly I understood the meaning of "aura." She wandered, marking each step with the swing of a spear and trailing her solar light across the field like a shadow defiant of its expected nature. Where she passed, the blood pooled, amassing and shifting until it sat upon the ground with solidity and took on the form and colour of fruit. She reached down and took a heart-shaped peach, blood running in a rivulet down her shining skin when she bit into it. The sun in the sky moved with her, framing her in a halo of the very essence of life and declaring her a being of sovereignty. Fecundity gushes forth from her passing, with each step sending a root of life into the Earth that will reach immediately for the nourishment of the light, acorn to oak in a heartbeat.

Then with a turn of her head, the sun dimmed, as though moving behind the clouds of her deep eyes and as she raised her spear for another step, she moved toward me.

Her arm became a flutter of black feathers, then a storm of black bird-life, enveloping me like a cloak of midnight storm, the lightning too distant for the sound of thunder to reach me with only the rapid rasp of feathers on feathers as my world thickened, darkened, became the depth of decay; became nothing. Nothing but her lips. A whisper in the folds of her embrace spoke of honour, spoke of courage, of pain and of love. A whisper in the womb of our espousal sung me back to life.

Hymn I to the Morrigan
by Valiel Elentári

Sometimes in front
Sometimes behind
Lies a mystery
Beyond my grasp

She's there by daylight
She's there at night
As my following shadow

I do call her
I try to reach her
But all in vain

She is the one who summons
She chooses to send messages
As She is the one who knows

She is true wisdom
She sees the whole picture
Goddess of Revelation

Hymn II to the Morrigan
by Valiel Elentári

Without a face
Or with too many
She's a wonder
Source of mystery

She wanders across the land
The land of darkness
Which few dare enter
Where few dare follow

Her black mantel upon her shoulders
Black errand upon shadow
She's a puzzling figure
Of the Night.

Banshee
by Ashley R. Bryner

They are hung in the hundreds.
She has counted each one.
Polished swords and spectacles
A worn jersey, burnished shields,
Bomber jackets, and baby bonnets
litter the thicket of blackthorns
A motley of unusual birds tangled among the branches
Newly washed and readied for the reunion that awaits them.
She remembers every name.

The grey-faced washer beats a white knuckled rhythm
The song of heartbeat and bone
Scouring until red blood runs clear
And is carried away in the current
Memories float away to the waters that birthed them.
Each button a shiny pearl.
Another wash cycle complete.

From the river she is drawn by distant cries of anguish
She pins her cloak around her and wanders
Light footfalls on the grass
The mother seeking her child,
A heavy heart her anchor, tears blown away
The wind rattles and shakes to herald her arrival
The veil between worlds glitters in her eyes.

Though grief labors her breathing and catches in her throat,
she throws back her head
and screams.
She cries with the voice of the crows, a crackling caw.

She sings with the voice of the mother, with no peace in her heart.
She mourns with the voice of those bereft of the child she has taken.
Downcast eyes espy her shrouded figure
A terrible cyclone of fabric and death.
Her beautiful face twisted in sorrow,
She cradles what remains of the young man so loved.
shrouding him in the shirt she has labored to clean,
And holds him there, tightly, until he is gone from her
A spirit carried aloft by her crows over the sea.
To join the others she has sent on.

Alone, she combs back her wild hair,
A jeweled gift from long ago
to remind her of better days.
Counting the toll of the dead of earth
Human, plant, animal alike.
Her work goes on forever.
Dark mother,
grey and crimson.
She remembers their names.

Nemain ~ Queen of the Battle Frenzy
by Vivienne Moss

Nemain, wife of the battle god Neit, is the Goddess of Battle Frenzy. Shrieking across the battlefields, Nemain rouses Her warriors with the strength and cunning to win the fight against their foes. If you are Her foe, Her banshee-like cry will cause your untimely death.

Little is known of Nemain. She is equated with Badb in the Tain Bo Cuailnge; "Nemain, which is Badb". Both are battle goddesses and both are married to Neit. It may be that they are the same. Many gods have more than one name, most being titles. I see them as two very different entities.

Nemain's name means "venomous," or "frenzy." Both conjure images of a very brutal woman. One you would not want to cross. For those who serve Her, She is a fierce protector. For Her foes, death is imminent. You can feel Her presence when confronted with a very dark, menacing anger. The type of anger you feel when you are confronted with danger or when you are diving into action to protect the innocent.

There are a few times in my life that I have felt Nemain's presence. The most poignant is when I was a teenager. I was down in the woods, riding one of our horses, when I heard my Mom and a male voice arguing. My Mom sounded distressed so I raced up the hill to see what was going on. My Uncle was there, my Mom's only sibling. He was yelling at her for reasons that are absurd. I could tell he had been drinking and wasn't in his right frame of mind. Suddenly, he took a step toward my Mom. I felt as if he were going to strike her. I don't know how I did it so quickly, but within seconds, I had jumped off my horse, handed the reins to my Mom and grabbed the pitch fork that had been leaning against the barn. With a scream, I pointed my weapon at my Uncle and chased him all the way to his truck. Telling him to get the fuck off our property and to never do that to my Mom again. As my Uncle drove away in a trail of dust, I walked back to my Mom and horse. I was still shaking, but very relieved that he had left without further incident. I think that might have been the first time my Mom had ever heard me say a curse word. I was very thankful she didn't scold me.

I believe Nemain was with me that day, giving me the courage and strength to stand up to my Uncle and protect my Mother. Years later, while sitting in the local pub having a beer with my Uncle, we talked about that day. Surprisingly, he could remember it. He told me that my eyes had turned red and he truly thought I was going to stab him with the pitch fork. I hate to think of what I would have done if he had hurt my Mom. Thankfully, all turned out for the good.

You know Nemain has entered your life when you feel the intense urge to take up battle. Whether it's to protect a loved one or to take a stand for a cause. She is not just a goddess for bloody wars, though She certainly can be called on by our brothers and sisters in uniform. She is the ultimate fighter for what is right and just in this world and the worlds beyond. Let Nemain fight by your side. Filling you with the battle frenzy you need to succeed. She and Her Sisters will stand with you if the cause is just. Like the Greek Nemesis, Goddess of justice, Nemain wields Her mighty sword, bringing vengeance and truth.

Call on the Great Warrioress Nemain when in need of protection or strength. She will come to those She deems worthy. Build an altar to Her displaying items of war and combat. Swords, daggers and spears would be appropriate. The colors of red and black should be used. Any herb for protection can be burned and offered to Nemain. I have found raptors and wolves to be sacred to Nemain. Working with their Spirits can be very beneficial.

I am thankful for the times Nemain has flown into my life. Like a Screaming Banshee, She has enticed me to stand up for myself and others. I am honored to feel Her presence embrace me.

Invocation to Nemain
by Vivienne Moss

Battle Fury
Fierce Warrior
Venomous One
Nemain, wife of Neit
I am in Your service
Fighting for what is true and just

Nemain
Filled with Frenzy
You entice those who battle for You
Giving them strength
And honor

Nemain
Vengeful One
Your foes drop like flies
Rotting for Crows to feast upon

Nemain
I am Your loyal servant
Use me as You will
To fight for the innocent
To protect the Children of Earth
And the Worlds Beyond …

Nemain
Battle Fury
Venomous One
Queen of the Battle Fields
Encircle me with your wrath
So I may fight alongside You

Reign
by S. E. Acker

The shadows hold her,
Their dearest child

She whispers,
Beyond the threshold of time

Born of Battle

Taker of souls

Cunning Lady of Shifting Form

She casts you asunder,
Into the deep

Queen of Dreams

Raven of Prophecy

Catch her thread,
Pulling at your heart

She will crown you there
Inside that tomb.

The Morrigan ~ My Queen
by Vivienne Moss

On the wings of the Raven She came to me
Calling me softly on the cool Autumn breeze
Wrapping me in Her dark embrace
The kiss of death on Her lips
The hope of life in Her eyes ...

The Morrigan, Mother of All
Queen of Elphame
Sovereign Queen of the mighty lands
Witch Mother, Mama Death
Queen of Shades and Shadows ...

I join You in the Dance Macabre
To learn
To fly
To explore
The worlds beyond ...

Calling, cawing
The cry of crows
The howl of wolves
The screech of owls
The bats' silent flight ...

I hear You
I feel You
I see You
I fear You
I love You

The Morrigan
My Queen
My Mother
My Destiny
My Truth ...

You have called
Through the darkness of night
Through the chant of spells
Through the death-like trance
I am ready ...

To fight
For honor
Glory
Truth
And wisdom ...

Morrigan
I am yours
In life
In death
For eternity ...

Morrigan
by Morgaine Nightshade

Nine Times Eternal:
The Ongoing Transformations of the Great Queen
by L. Sixfingers

The Great Queen has survived through the ages and in these days, we might even begin to say that She has come to the outskirts of time when She will thrive again. Yet, it has never been our place, as storytellers and writers, priestesses and warriors, to tell the Great Queen much of anything She does not already know. We hope as Her devotees, feral children, and co-conspirators to pull forth from the darkness, the greening places, and our own beautiful spirits some sparks of ever-changing truth to set us alight. What I have experienced of the Mórrígan is that She is now and has always been a multi-cultural, multi-racial, and multi-ethnic Goddess who has traveled the worlds extensively. Her battle cry is far-reaching and She is calling to us beyond boundaries of race, culture, gender, and sexuality, meeting the complex needs of modern Pagans and Polytheists with diverse identities.

We experience the Mórrígan in a myriad of ways. As raven, crow, wolf, and eel; as shadow, warrior, priestess, and hag; sometimes kind, sometimes frenzied, other times beyond human emotion. I recognize the Mórrígan as a single Goddess, as nine separate Goddesses, as three sets of nine Goddessses, and at some point a few years ago, as She appeared to me more readily in a form that was human, She looked more like the womyn[1] of my community and all its diversity. I realized then how She had survived for so many centuries when other God/desses had not fared so well - She had traveled far and wide and followed us, Her raven children, to all edges of the

---

[1] For me, the term *womyn* describes a gender and cultural identity that is binary-free and self-determined.

earth, Her bloodline expanding, becoming many-tongued, and talented in the art of connecting cultures.

I should be clear that I am a panentheist – I believe that the Gods are both wholly separate and completely immanent at all times. I believe we are the Gods and the Gods are also Something Else (which in turn makes us Something Else). I am comfortable with this paradox and it has been, in part, what has driven me to write about the Mórrígan in such a way that includes folks like me who are queer, multi-ethnic, multi-racial, multi-cultural, and resolutely one of Her own. My proposal is this – the Mórrígan as a shapeshifter, as a survivor, and as a Goddess whose expressions are limitless, is a multi-cultural, multi-racial, multi-species creature who has remained relevant because of Her diversity. We need God/desses who look and talk and act like us – just as we need God/desses who are terribly Other and frighteningly strange. It has been my experience that the Mórrígan is both at the same time – a reflection of our diverse world and an incomprehensible creature veiled in deepening mystery.

The Mórrígan's diverse roots appear as early as the invasion of Ireland by the people of Nemed. Nemed, descended of the Greeks of ancient Scythia, landed in Ireland with his followers and offspring, as the third invasion in the mythological cycle of the *Lebor Gabála Érenn*. After two centuries and a terrible plague, in which Nemed died, as well as oppressive rule by the Fomorians, the last of Nemedians left Ireland for good. The Tuatha Dé Danaan, of whom the Mórrígan is part of, are descended from Nemed and his offspring. It was the Nemedians who traveled back to Greece and also up North to learn the art of "pagan cunning," their offspring becoming the Tuatha Dé Danaan who eventually returned to Ireland.[2] While these are mythological cycles with

---

[2] Macalister, Robert Alexander Stewart, trans. *Lebor Gabála Erenn*. Dublin: Irish Texts Society, 1938. 92. Print.

bits of truth thrown in for good measure, I think it is important to note that there exists an early multicultural heritage (Greek, Irish, Scythian, and the mysterious northern lands) that the Mórrígan is descended from.

Through continued invasion by the Milesians, the Romans, and then Christianization of Ireland (let us mourn the day the snakes were driven out), the Mórrígan has survived – as Goddess, Faery, hag, a sister to the King, Lover, Priestess, and an enchantress. In my work with the Mórrígan, I understand Her as a nine-fold Goddess and I have continued to explore ways of experiencing Her complexity in the midst of our own modern complexities of identity – especially in places like North America where a hostile overculture[3] actively oppresses anything not in line with a happy, white, middle-class, straight, able-bodied, monotheistic image of normalcy. In my practice with the Mórrígan, I have developed my own names and attributes for each of the nine faces of the Mórrígan in an attempt to describe the ways that expresses Her limitlessness and how She continues to influence the worlds.[4] These attributes and names are not meant to be understood as complete and separate identities – just as we are complex creatures with overlapping interests and skill sets, so too has been the experience of most of the Goddesses I have ever encountered. She is a warrior in all that She does and She is also

---

[3] "Overculture" is a term I was first exposed to through the writings of Joy Harjo of the Mvskoke Nation. Overculture describes an artificial, oppressive, and colonial "culture" based on materialism and power-over that disconnects us from one another.

[4] Thanks to John and Caitlin Matthews whose work *Ladies of the Lake* inspired the idea of the nine-point star as an image of the Mórrígan. Matthews, Caitlin, and John Matthews. *Ladies of the Lake*. London: Aquarian, 1992. Print.

lover and healer, a seer and mother of earth and bones, crone of prophecy, and any multitude of Her animal forms.

The names and their attributes are guidelines, not ultimatums – ongoing poetic interpretation rather than a completed work. I have used some traditional Irish names of the Mórrígan but have avoided describing Her with only traditional attributes. When She does appear to me in human form She is often of womyn of many races, ethnicities, and cultures and She reflects that in Her physical qualities. I encourage you to work with the following information in ritual and devotional work, continuing the conversation of Who and What the Mórrígan is and in turn, Who and What we are. It has been my experience that the work with the Mórrígan is always in-process, ever-revealing, turning and spiraling like the tattoos along Her skin, like the rivers of her blood, and the song of Her mighty sorcery and battle cry.

The Nine Faces of the Mórrígan

The **Activist** spurs us to action. She is the restoration of energy when all hope seems lost and she is also present at every new idea, every beginning, every sudden breakthrough insight. She is the first to run into the fray and she is the ecstasy of hearts split open in courageous joy. I call Her Fódla, the leader of faery hordes, the One Who greeted the Milesians as they came to Ireland's shore, being an incarnation of Ireland (Ériu) itself. An activist is tied to something – some passion, some great drive and calling to better the world – and so Fódla is tied to the earth as one incarnation of the land itself, unafraid to step forward on the land's (and her) behalf with her wild band of Good Folk.

As **Intermediary**, Badb meets us at our edges as we are just about to make the next move in our journey. She mediates between this world and the next and the next beyond that one. She is often found at the gates between life and death as the Washer at the Ford and the hooded crows on the battlefield of the dying. Her skill as mediator helps us to reconcile all of our experiences as people: as people of color, as queer folks, as differently-abled, poor, rich, middling, multi-ethnic, and the myriad of expressions of our humanness. Badb is the one to call when the stagnant decay of outmoded habits and institutionalized oppression prevents true and growing relationships from prospering – She is the red-mouthed bean-sídhe who sings of the fall of empires as well as prophetess of peace eternal.

The **Warrior** would probably be the most familiar aspect of the Mórrígan to many and She has certainly been immortalized in early Irish literature as a loathsome and warlike hag, who stalks the battlefield and its warriors. The Mórrígan's appearance as the Warrior is inescapably gruesome - raining down "mighty showers of fire, and a downpour of red blood" on the Fir Bolgs[5] and killing men with the very sound of Her voice calling warriors to battle.[6] Yet, while She is a formidable foe on the battlefield, She is ultimately a teacher and defender of boundaries that have been set to protect the integrity of the land and its people. She is a disruptive force to those who are foolhardy, thinking only of themselves and their personal glory (embodied in the Táin Bó Cúailnge by the warrior Cú Chulainn), reminding them in sometimes cruel, but always enlightening ways, of the lesson of interconnectedness. I call Her Macha, who is both an instigator of battle as well as a Goddess of sovereignty and who cursed the Ulsterman for their inhumanity - for making Her race against horses during her ninth month of pregnancy all for the purpose of defending personal pride. She reminds us that we stand on the backs of those who came before and we fight for the future of our descendents.

  Before it has come to pass, the **Seer** has seen it, and so the Mórrígan acts as initiatory visionary, prophesying both war and peace. As Seer, I call Her Nemain who is described as "of prophetic stanzas" and often plays the role of a **bean-sídhe**.[7] Nemain's names has been translated as "Frenzy" which is usually understood as a reference to "battle frenzy," but as someone who does a lot of trancework, I feel it is appropriate to also consider that Nemain's frenzy could be of a prophetic form as well. When the path seems uncertain and even impossible, the Seer offers insight, shattering expectation and barriers

---

[5] Fraser, John. "The Battle of Moytura Or, The First Battle of Magh Turedh." *Celtic Literature Collective.* Mary Jones, n.d. Web. 28 July 2012. <http://www.maryjones.us/ctexts/1maghtured.html>

[6] Kinsella, Thomas. *The Táin: Translated from the Irish Epic Táin Bó Cuailnge.* Oxford: Oxford University, 1970. Print.

[7] Macalister, Robert Alexander Stewart. *Lebor Gabála Erenn.* 216.

erected by our own insecurity and societal restrictions. She also does the work of dreaming the future, uncovering hidden his/herstories, and creating passageways between times and places.

As **Crisis**, the Mórrígan can be terrifying for She appears when we must strip away all that does not serve us which is usually what is most familiar and ingrained in our sense of self. Identity crisis, healing crisis, quarter-life and midlife crisis, and Saturn returns are the time of the Mórrígan as Crisis, who I call Fea. Fea's name is sometimes translated as "Hateful One" which can describe the feeling of hate and disgust we hold for ourselves and our perceived inadequacies within an overculture that demands impossible standards of so-called "perfection." The Crisis can be personal, relational, local, and global – the energy crisis, global warming crisis, financial crisis are all the domains of Fea. At first it seems She appears to be our adversary, but She is only enemy to illusions which keep us captive and which we believe to be in our best interest but are not. She curates a certain chaos that through Crisis we may find regeneration, facing our fears and weaknesses, and drawing strength from the journey of pulling through.

The **Healer** is an important aspect of the Mórrígan, working closely with Crisis. For me the aspect of Healer has always appeared as the Avalonian Priestess Morgan Le Fay,[8] one of the Mórrígan's most human aspects. Where there is suffering, She is there, just as She hovers as the hooded crow

---

[8] Not a traditional Irish name for the Mórrígan and some find the equating of the two figures to be incorrect, uninformed, and at the very least, irritating. While a much longer paper is needed to explore the two figures and their relationship, I have my own reasons for including Morgan Le Fay as a title of the Mórrígan which include personal experience and the experience of my wider community with the Mórrígan. The myths shift and are still being written... Let us not forget they are only stories, still sacred and meaningful, but tales that are not only meant to be retold but undone, re-membered, and future dreamed.

over the battlefield and over the dying King Arthur. I believe that Morgan le Fay serves as a title, in addition to describing a single Priestess and Goddess, which describes the otherworldly healers of the Isle of Women. At death She ushers us to a place of respite before our reincarnation and throughout life we can continuously call on Her transformative powers to relieve us of our every burden. I think that John and Caitlín Matthews accurately describe the gifts of the Healer as "when we are able to go beyond our own selfishness into a wider compassion, when we refuse to pass our pain onto others."[9]

The **Weaver** works the web of all the worlds, the many-formed Witch and shapeshifter who dwells within all the worlds. I call the Weaver by the name the Mórrígan because She is the woven collective of each individual identity that She possesses – at once both many and one. It is the Weaver, through all Her complex compositions who reveals to us the unique calling which is all our own. The Weaver is the "source of enchantment" from which all magick is conceived.[10] While able to reveal to us our individuality, the Mórrígan emphasizes that we are still woven together with the rest of all that is, was, and shall be. To work with the Mórrígan as Weaver is to walk in the world as a Priest/ess and to uphold the vows of complexity and the compassion to match it.

The Mórrígan also possesses a parental aspect who I call the **Guardian** and name as Banba. Banba as the Guardian is the land come to life, an Earth Goddess who both seeks wild spaces and is also the embodiment of earth left for the pleasure of itself, as Her name means "unplowed field." Through Her myths and my own work with Her, I find Banba to be particularly interested in womyn's culture, reminding us that

---

[9] Matthews, Caitlin, and John Matthews. *Ladies of the Lake*. London: Aquarian, 1992. Print.

[10] Macalister, Robert Alexander Stewart. *Lebor Gabála Erenn*. 216.

Ireland was once a land of womyn when She first settled it. Banba may also be seen as the Isle of Avalon, Her Guardian energies shielding the mysteries with a thick mist. She is the one to call on when a safe-space is needed for those who need restoration from the isolation of the overculture and to be able to dream a new culture that is more just and kind. At Her core, the Guardian is our very practice, the traditions we keep, and the rites we work. Banba is the source of enchantment made manifest as root, rock, and bone. To work with the Guardian is to become intoxicated with land and its mysteries, to experience the Mórrígan as lover and Her unending pleasure.

Manifesting as the **Advocate**, the Mórrígan promotes a sustainable network of inclusion, which recognizes that a culture is only as strong as its growing wild edges where diversity of experience flourishes. The Advocate is Danu, Mother of the Gods, Who is Sovereignty and Certainty. Danu is the stillness of balance, when you know what you have and you know what you must give, and the courage to fight for something bigger than your own survival. The Advocate infuses our work with purpose and clarity, as Danu is our very heartbeat and the pause between inhalation and exhalation. When we work long hours organizing on the behalf of others, taking to the streets, loving bravely, and dismantling oppressive structures of power-over, Danu is our drumbeat and the unending rhythm that carries us through.

Invocation of the Great Queen
Hail to the Great Queen
Nine Times Eternal

To Fódla
The Activist
Courageous joy
The ecstasy of service
Hail to the Great Queen
nine times eternal

To Badb
The Intermediary
Rich of experience
Present at the edges
Hail to the Great Queen
nine times eternal

To Macha
The Warrior
Defender of boundaries
Integrity of lineage
Hail to the Great Queen
nine times eternal

To Nemain
The Seer
Initiatory visions
Frenzied passage
Hail to the Great Queen
nine times eternal

To Fea
The Crisis
Trial of regeneration
Curator of chaos
Hail to the Great Queen
nine times eternal

To Morgan le Fay
The Healer
Priestess of Avalon
Island of respite
Hail to the Great Queen
nine times eternal

To the Mórrígan
The Weaver
Source of enchantment
Complexity of compassion
Hail to the Great Queen
nine times eternal

To Banba
The Guardian
Space of solace
Pleasure of wildness
Hail to the Great Queen
nine times eternal

To Danu
The Advocate
The flourishing heart
The beat of connection
Peace to sky
sky to earth
be this nine times eternal

Words Of The Morrigan
by Raven Spirit

When the winter winds doth blow, you will hear my call
I am the mother of the brave, and will catch you when you fall
I am the goddess of battles long, and struggles that run deep
When the fighting is over, you are the prize you keep
You will see me as the bird most look upon as ill
But in the heart of my child the raven brings a thrill
I am the Queen of prophecy and things yet unknown
But look within your deepest heart for there all things are
    shown
I walk the pathway between life and death, the sword is in my
    hand
I strike the final and deadly blow, spilling blood upon the land
But don't think me harsh, or cold, for that is not my way
I sit and weep at the ford, washing the blood away
You are my child and I your Queen, when you take my hand
At the end of time, and your days, I will lead you to
    Summerland

Morrigan Above Stonehenge
by Morgaine Nightshade

A Testimonal
by Copper Moon

It was June 1981, and my family and I were leaving my grandparents' home in England to come home from our holiday. I was about twelve years-old at the time. As we were heading to get into our rental car, a lady's voice told me, 'Go back to your Granddad and tell him that you love him, and give him a hug'. I didn't think anything of it at the time. I didn't stop to question who this lady was nor where the voice came from. I just turned around and waved to him and told him that I loved him. By the end to the next month he was diagnosed with pancreatic cancer. He passed away at the end of that November -- the day after his birthday. I didn't know it then, but it was the Morrigan who spoke to me. And she's been with me for as long as I can remember in some shape or form over the years.

Most people think of blood, guts, and battle when they hear of this beautiful goddess. I've always had the prophesy aspects of Morrigan shown to me in the guise of Badb or the bean si. I've not always listened to these whisperings in my younger days, but have come to appreciate them more along my path. If nothing else, I've learned to be true to myself and listen within -- She will guide me when in a quandry and ensure I learn what I need to know to make myself a better person. Morrigan has also taught me to embrace fear, for that is what makes me stronger.

The Morrígan and Cú Chulainn: A More Nuanced View of Their Relationship
by P. Sufenas Virius Lupus

For a modern polytheist reconstructionist, the very concept of the Morrígan presents a number of problems. While she does act as an individual goddess under the name "the Morrígan" in a variety of Irish tales, her name is also used for a class of divine beings, and she is said to be the sister of Badb and Macha (and there are at least three Machas in Irish myth as well!), or sometimes Badb, Macha, and Némain are said to be "the Morrígna" as a group (or "Morrígan" might substitute for one of those names in the collective triplicate group). Likewise, she is also said to be called Ana (genitive Anann) or Dana (genitive Danann), and thus equivalent to the goddess that many modern pagans worship as Danu; and, she is also identified in one text with Bé Néit, the wife of the god Nét (or, alternately, simply "woman of battle"), who is elsewhere said to be Némain.[1] In this respect, the Morrígan as a modern goddess for pagan and polytheist devotion is in a similar position to Brigit, who is clearly described as a triplicity of goddesses in medieval Irish sources, but she tends to be taken as a singular goddess persona (combining in several other figures from Irish and Scottish narrative called Bríg or Bríd, as well as the diverse traditions around St. Brigit of Kildare and other saints called Brigit), possibly with multiple aspects, forms, or manifestations. Whether both of these phenomena are due to an evolving intra-pantheonic syncretistic reality,[2] or if this instead reflects the variability and freedom of the medieval Irish monastic scholars and authors, or (perhaps least optimistically, but nonetheless realistically) this simply demonstrates the lack of critical attention, good information, and the general laziness and apathy around discovering what Irish sources actually say about particular deities amongst modern pagans and polytheists, is a matter of one's own opinion for the most part.

While there is, thus, some controversy over the identity of the Morrígan, so to speak, it is not surprising that there are varying interpretations of her role within many medieval Irish narratives, and what her overall function is within an Irish (or more widely Gaelic) polytheistic pantheon. Nonetheless, some of the most erroneous and inappropriate ideas about the Morrígan come from the stories of her interactions with the great Ulster Cycle hero Cú Chulainn, and expectations put upon their apparent conflict which are not remotely applicable to their situations or their places in the literature and mythology more widely. It is the intent of the present discussion to shed some light on how problematic these interpretations are, and to come to a more nuanced and appropriate view of the great war-goddess the Morrígan's relationship to the paragon of warrior virtue in Irish tradition, Cú Chulainn, based on the actual medieval sources as they stand and as they were written, rather than through modern, misinformed interpretive lenses.

In order to understand these matters, we must first examine the main incident from which these erroneous interpretations arise. This is the incident in the Ulster Cycle epic *Táin Bó Cúailnge*, "The Cattle-Raid of Cooley,"[3] in which the Morrígan comes to Cú Chulainn in disguise as a beautiful woman, the daughter of Búan the king, and offers her help and sexual favors to the hero, and he refuses, which only occurs in recension I of the narrative.[4] At one point in their conversation, Cú Chulainn very plainly states, "*Ní ar thóin mná dano gabus-sa inso,*"[5] which roughly translates as "It is not for the sake of a woman's cunt that I have come [on this foray]!"[6] What follows is the Morrígan's attack against Cú Chulainn while he is fighting his foster-brother Lóch Mór mac Emonis, with the goddess taking the forms of an eel, a red heifer, and a grey wolf, which occurs in three recensions of the *Táin*,[7] and then Cú Chulainn's eventual healing of her afterwards when she takes the form of a wounded old woman offering him milk. The incident of the serial shapeshifting is also foretold in another Irish cattle-raid tale, *Táin Bó Regamna*, when the goddess comes to drive a particular important cow in an odd chariot with a charioteer, and then becomes a raven for her final pronouncement to the hero;[8] and, this tale is briefly alluded to further in the story *Echtra Nerai*.[9]

The prevailing pagan view of this matter, found endlessly repeated across the internet and in some less well-informed publications, is that Cú Chulainn's death eventually results directly because the Morrígan avenged herself against him for this refusal, in her capacity not only as a war-goddess, but also as the sovereignty goddess. This is erroneous for a variety of reasons, including that as early as the "Boyhood Deeds of Cú Chulainn" in *Táin Bó Cúailnge*, Cú Chulainn sets out on his first warrior foray as a child knowing full well that if he does so on that particular day, he will have a short life but be famed forever after for his warrior prowess.[10] That there are so many independent Irish narrative texts that presage the shapeshifted fight of the Morrígan with Cú Chulainn during the course of the great cattle-raid, and that the conflict between them arises only in recension I due to her refused advances is thus a minority tradition that cannot be read as a universal or an implied understanding across other texts (especially including Cú Chulainn's death tale's various versions), is an aspect of this matter that has not been properly accounted for in any pagan or polytheist treatment of the issue that has come to my attention. But, the notion that the Morrígan here (and elsewhere) is acting in the role of the sovereignty goddess is a noteworthy misreading which should be addressed.

A common theme in Irish mythology is for a prospective king of Ireland, often during the course of a hunt and looking for shelter or water, comes into the presence of the Goddess of Sovereignty (always revealed to be such, with no other names given for her), who offers him water in return for sexual favors.

Would-be kings who are not fit for rulership always refuse her, but the true king-to-be gladly accepts, and his future fate is revealed afterwards.[11] This pattern is perhaps most famously established in the tale about Niall of the Nine Hostages,[12] founder of the Uí Néill dynasty of Irish kings which lasted for the majority of the medieval period, who establishes his relationship with the Sovereignty Goddess where all of his brothers (and the more logically apparent heirs of the kingship as his elders and legitimate sons of king Eochaid Mugmedóin) fail. What often happens in such tales, however, is that the Sovereignty Goddess initially appears old and hideous to the prospective king, but after a kiss or sexual intercourse is exchanged between them, the Sovereignty Goddess becomes radiantly beautiful.

Thus, first and foremost, it must be noted that in the situation with the Morrígan and Cú Chulainn in the *Táin*'s first recension, this is not the pattern at all, since she first appears to him as a beautiful young woman, then reveals her true nature after her refusal, becomes three animal shapes in their next encounter, and then appears finally as an old and wounded hag seeking not sexual favors, but instead blessings from the hero in order to be healed. Second, the Goddess of Sovereignty offers one thing and one thing only to her prospective mates: rightful kingship of the land, even though she might appear to be a keeper of a well and a giver of water, and her offer of the rightful kingship's confirmation is not announced or previously implied to the prospective king. This is, again, not the offer that the Morrígan in the form of Búan the king's daughter makes to Cú Chulainn: she specifically offers love and wealth and her sexual favors, and only offers her assistance in the battle after his initial refusal. Third, the Goddess of the Sovereignty of Ireland, in all extant literatures featuring her, is never given another name. While modern scholars have interpreted various Irish mythological characters, both mortal and divine, as exemplifying the Sovereignty Goddess, it is to be understood that these are modern interpretations, and are not stated within the medieval texts themselves.[13] Fourth and finally for the moment, Cú Chulainn could never be a realistic contestant for Sovereignty's favor, because he is "blemished" due to his battle-fury and the distortion upon his body which it brings, whereas rightful kings must be whole and healthy and have no physical blemishes or imperfections about them. Though Cú Chulainn is regarded as being superlatively beautiful, a statement in the tale *Tochmarc Emire* indicates that he had undescended testicles, which most certainly would disqualify him for the kingship as well.[14]

The notion that the Morrígan is a "Sovereignty Goddess" in itself needs some re-evaluation (which will be undertaken further below), but that she grants her favors in battle via sexual liaisons comes from her function in *Cath Maige Tuired*. In this text, she is said to have arranged a tryst with the Dagda near (note, not "on") the date of the festival of Samain before the great battle of the Túatha Dé with the Fomoiri, whereupon she advises on the troop movements of the Fomoiri, and says she will specifically debilitate Indech mac Dé Domnann of the Fomoiri in the battle.[15] It is to be noted in this incident that, likewise, the Dagda is neither the king of the Túatha Dé at the time, nor is he a candidate for that position in the run-up to the battle, and thus concerns over sovereignty are irrelevant to the situation. Just after this part of the text, the Dagda goes to spy on the Fomoiri, enjoys their hospitality in an immense feast, and then afterwards has a sexual encounter with Indech's daughter.[16] This incident often gets elided and combined into the encounter of the Dagda with the Morrígan, and they become conflated, but they are two entirely different incidents, though they have somewhat similar results. The bombastic scene in which the Dagda gets Indech's daughter to say his full name, is humiliated in various ways, and then succumbs to her sexual advances, is followed by her demand that he not go to the battle, and she threatens to impede him in the form of a stone and a great oak tree amidst every ford he will cross, but he says those things will not stop his resolve, whereupon she says she will help him in the battle and advises him on strategy. Her threats (never realized) of shapeshifting and impeding him in the ford is far more comparable to the (realized) threats of the Morrígan of shapeshifting into animal forms in the ford battle against Cú Chulainn, but the similarities end there, since the Morrígan's threats result from Cú Chulainn's refusal of her sexual advances, whereas the Dagda has already granted his sexual favors to Indech's daughter when she makes the threats that never come to pass.

Another suggestion about Cú Chulainn's enmity with the Morrígan being roused with the result that she brings about his death is that in the death-tale of Cú Roí, *Aided Con Roi*, Cú Chulainn kills a number of blackbirds during the course of his journey to find Cú Roí.[17] As Badb and/or the Morrígan, transformation into corvids of various sorts is a frequent occurrence, and thus Cú Chulainn's targeting of blackbirds has been considered an offense to her by some. There is no indication, however, that this is the case at all. The story of Cú Chulainn's killing of the birds is used as a typical *dindshenchas* ("lore of famous places") tale, to simply give the origins of the placename Srub Brain, "Raven's Beak," which is attested in many other Irish tales as a place where significant actions occurred.

This brings us to the actual death of Cú Chulainn itself, and the incident which has drawn the most attention in the overall formation of the erroneous portrait of the hero's relationship with the Morrígan: namely, her appearance as a crow that alights on his shoulder after his death, as if she has at last achieved victory over the hero.[18] While this corvid alighting incident certainly does occur in the oldest version of his death-tale as it is currently preserved, there is no indication in the text as it stands that the scald-crow that so alights upon his shoulder after his death is, in fact, the Morrígan herself (or Badb, or any other goddess in an avian form); there is nothing to suggest at all that the bird is magical, supernatural, or a transformed deity of any sort. Thus, this is an interpretation that has been put upon the text which the text itself does not seem to support. In every other case when the goddess appears in avian form, her shapeshifting into that form and her divine reality behind such apparent avian appearances is plainly indicated;[19] thus an exception here would have to be justified via some means that has not been forthcoming previously.

Another set of occasions occurs in which it has been misinterpreted (both by scholars and by some modern practitioners) that the Morrígan appears is in *Brislech Mór Maige Múirthemne*, a kind of fore-tale to Cú Chulainn's death-tale proper, where a woman called Badb changed shape to appear as the Ulsterwoman Niamh and to encourage Cú Chulainn to go on his final foray in which his death would occur.[20] However, this "Badb" is not the goddess Badb, but instead one of the children of Calatín Dána, who had been killed in the *Táin* by Cú Chulainn, and whose children were involved in avenging their father's death in collaboration with Medb. These children do manage to bring about Cú Chulainn's death in the later tale, especially when they appear as three one-eyed old women who offer the hero dog-meat, which he cannot refuse, and which weakens him considerably before his final battle.[21] The common misconstruction that these three dog-roasting women were in league with the Morrígan, or that one (or more) of them were the goddess herself, is a further modern interpretation which has no basis in the medieval texts. Further, a "washer at the ford" also appears to presage the death of the hero in this tale, who is identified as "Badb's daughter."[22] It seems more likely that this is the goddess Badb (possibly identical with the Morrígan), rather than Badb the daughter of Calatín Dána mentioned earlier; and if that is indeed the case, then it seems that the Morrígan/Badb here is more in sympathy with the hero rather than wishing to bring about his death or being involved in killing him.

However, the Morrígan very definitely does appear in Cú Chulainn's death tale, quite briefly toward the beginning before he sets out on his fateful final foray. It is worth quoting the translation of this incident in full in order to achieve clarity on the goddess' role in the proceedings. "And the Morrígan had broken [Cú Chulainn's] chariot the night before; for she did not wish Cú Chulainn to go to the battle, for she knew that he would not come back to Emain Macha."[23] It need not be stated any more fancifully or honorably than that: the Morrígan did not wish for the hero to die, even though it was fated by his own actions to occur when he was young, and on that very specific particular occasion that was about to occur. Even the goddess of battle herself, it seems, cannot dispute the final fate of a great hero, though she apparently does wish she could have prevented it. This plainly indicates that she had sympathy and admiration for the hero, not enmity or spite and a wish for vengeance, as has so often been stated.

Two matters remain to be treated in brief in terms of fully understanding the correct interpretation of the incident in *Táin Bó Cúailnge*'s first recension between Cú Chulainn and his refusal of the Morrígan's sexual favors: first, the status of the Morrígan as a goddess of sovereignty; and second, the ethical context for such a refusal.

The Morrígan's status as a sovereignty goddess is questioned, as we have seen above, by the lack of certain characteristics that accompany most traditional Sovereignty Goddess myths, as already discussed. The two incidents in which this is at all exhibited with her in the extant medieval Irish literary corpus are the scenes of successful mating with the Dagda from *Cath Maige Tuired*, and the failed attempt at such with Cú Chulainn in *Táin Bó Cúailnge*, both of which do not qualify as Sovereignty Goddess myths as such at all, thus invalidating this interpretation entirely. But, is there any possibility that she may have such a sovereignty connection at all?

I believe there is, and it is a matter which has to do with the etymology of her name. While the element *–rígain* in her name, meaning "queen," is obvious and unquestioned, the first element of her name has been more problematic. Sometimes, both in scholarship and in the medieval Irish texts as they stand, her name's first element is given as *Mór-*, which means "great," and hence the meaning "Great Queen" is understood for her name.

However, when it is given without an acute accent, the element of *Mor-* is the same as the middle element in the ethnonym "Fomoiri," the monstrous indigenous race that inhabits Ireland before any of the waves of subsequent invaders arrive on its shores, and who are defeated by the Túatha Dé in *Cath Maige Tuired*. Understanding her name under this form yields the translation of the Morrígan as "Phantom Queen" quite often in English. This element is derived from an Indo-European root, and has a meaning similar to the *–mare* in the English word "nightmare," not meaning "female equine," but instead "spirit/creature/monster."[24] As the Fomoiri are indigenous to the land of Ireland (though tales like *Cath Maige Tuired* seem to indicate they come from elsewhere), and in the earliest Leinster dynastic poetry, they are indistinguishable from any other race of deities or spirits that are said to exist within the *síd*-mounds of Ireland,[25] it might be good to understand their name as "under-spirits." Further, it would be useful to take this term as synonymous with other words in various cultures for "land spirits," which can be potentially beneficial if they are treated correctly, but which can also be antagonistic to humans—and, apparently, the race of the gods known as the Túatha Dé as well. Perhaps, thus, the Morrígan can be thought of as the queen of the land spirits of Ireland, which may or may not put her in relationship to the goddess of sovereignty, but which in itself would be a significant matter, given that various spirits of battle in Irish tradition are closely tied with the land itself.[26]

Secondly, the refusal of the Morrígan by Cú Chulainn in this incident has been judged very harshly by many modern pagan and polytheist practitioners: if a goddess offers her help, shouldn't one accept it? I've also heard more recent arguments that no one should refuse any sort of help when offered, and thus this incident serves as a negative exemplar of what befalls humans when they do not accept the freely-offered help of deities.

Beyond the obvious thought that Cú Chulainn refusing such help would have been a detriment to his honor as a self-confident and independent warrior hero, there is a further matter at stake here. As a warrior, the role of such figures is not to participate in acts of fertility or sexuality, but instead to deal in "anti-fertility," namely death. The forbidding of sexual relationships to youthful outlaw hunter-warriors, of which Cú Chulainn is most certainly a shining example, is relatively common in Indo-European (and other) cultures. The penalties for transgressing this sexual ethic are severe, and are exemplified best perhaps by a Graeco-Roman tale that is well-known: that of Aktaion/Actaeon, who desired the goddess Artemis/Diana, and paid with his life when he was transformed into a stag and was hunted and harried to his death by his own hounds.[27] It was not that he desired a goddess which earned him his death, or that Artemis was a sworn virgin, or even that he was intruding into private divine space, but instead that he was in a social state that prevented his forming of relationships of a sexual nature. As that particular social state also had sacred functions as constitutive parts of it, and was hemmed around with a variety of injunctions and taboos, the exemplary nature of the Actaeon myth demonstrates that this sort of behavior is not tolerated by the gods.

Conversely, Cú Chulainn's handling of the situation is exactly what it should have been, and even though the goddess threatens him and carries through on her threats, he still not only overcomes her, but goes on to even greater heights of heroic warrior prowess. When he encounters the goddess again and ends up healing her, there is very likely some resentment present, but none is expressed on her part, since she emerges from the situation no worse off than before. And, her final appearance in his life is to sabotage his chariot before his last battle, since she did not wish him to die.

What emerges, thus, in a closer examination of these incidents and their cultural relevance in wider Irish mythology, is that Cú Chulainn was not in any manner cursed or disfavored by the Morrígan, either in her potential role as a sovereignty goddess (since she was not acting in that capacity here, and he was not a realistic candidate for kingship anyway) or as a battle goddess. In fact, in that specific latter capacity, it appears that the goddess herself decided to test the hero's virtue by tempting him with sexual indulgence, which would have diminished his warrior ardor and would have endangered his province's protection by his absence and distraction. He proved himself worthy of his renown as a warrior hero with his refusal, and her engagement with him in animal shapes as an unfair incursion into his battle with Lóch was a further and more direct test of his warrior abilities, which he likewise passed with flying colors. His greatest warrior feats follow immediately, with his most intense and destructive battle-frenzy in the *Táin* occurring after the battle with Lóch, and then his fateful combat with his other foster-brother and lover Fer Diad following after that, which was itself the subject of the extended and more fully elaborated and vastly popular text, *Táin Bó Cúailnge* recension four. Cú Chulainn earned his position and honoring as a great warrior by passing these tests, administered by the goddess of battle herself, and earned his proper reward for it: eternal fame. Though she would have preferred to have had him around for longer, as the champion and protector of the Ulaid at Emain Macha, and to do even greater feats of battle under her patronage and for her own glory—as all warfare is to a goddess of warfare—he chose his death as much as he chose his path in life, and the Morrígan ultimately respected that.

Applying modern values and understandings of divine intervention, warfare, and appropriate interactions with deities to these tales is not relevant, and in fact fundamentally misunderstands their original contexts and the ideals which underlie these tales and are exemplified within them. It is as inappropriate to apply the standards of the typical sovereignty goddess tale to Cú Chulainn and the Morrígan, thus, as it would be to criticize a modern soldier in the U.S. Armed Forces for not upholding his destiny since that soldier did not create executive orders for the withdrawal of all troops from Afghanistan. It is important to always understand, when dealing with the realities of Irish mythic narrative, that the culture which produced these narratives is as different and often opposed to our own as can possibly be imagined. We do no honor nor devoted service to the deities and heroes involved if we impose our own values upon the interpretation or re-telling of these narratives in the modern period; indeed, in doing so, we might in fact be satirizing and demeaning the heroes, even if such intents were not at all in one's mind when doing so. But if we do decide to re-tell, re-interpret, and as a result refashion these tales, we should claim them as modern innovations and as novelties appropriate to our own times, and not as the inheritance of tradition nor as being within the lineage of our ancient and medieval spiritual ancestors.

Notes

1. Elizabeth A. Gray (ed./trans.), *Cath Maige Tuired: The Second Battle of Mag Tuired*, Irish Texts Society Vol. 52 (Dublin and London: Irish Texts Society, 1982), pp. 129-130.

2. For more on this variety of syncretism, see P. Sufenas Virius Lupus, *A Serpent Path Primer* (Anacortes: The Red Lotus Library, 2012), pp. 6-7.

3. *Táin Bó Cúailnge* exists in four recensions, and dates in its earliest portions to the seventh century CE; the oldest of the four recensions (known as Recension I) is found largely in the late-eleventh/early-twelfth-century manuscript *Lebor na hUidre*, while the second recension is found in its entirety in the twelfth-century *Book of Leinster*. The Morrígan only appears in the first three recensions of TBC, and the fourth recension does not currently exist in an edited form. *Recension I:* Cecile O'Rahilly (ed./trans.), *Táin Bó Cúailnge*, Recension I (Dublin: Dublin Institute for Advanced Studies, 1967). *Recension II:* Cecile O'Rahilly (ed./trans.), *Táin Bó Cualnge from the Book of Leinster* (Dublin: Dublin Institute for Advanced Studies, 1968); Cecile O'Rahilly (ed.), *The Stowe Version of Táin Bó Cuailnge* (Dublin: Dublin Institute for Advanced Studies, 1978).. *Recension III:* Max Nettlau (ed.), "The Fragment of the Táin Bó Cúailnge in MS. Egerton 93 (ff. 26a 1-35b 2)," *Revue Celtique 15* (1894), 62-78, 198-208; Pádraig Ó Fiannachta (ed.), *Táin Bó Cuailnge The Maynooth Manuscript* (Dublin: Dublin Institute for Advanced Studies, 1980); Feargal Ó Béarra (trans.), "Táin Bó Cuailnge: Recension III," Emania 15 (1996), pp. 47-65. Further reference to O'Rahilly's editions/translations of the first recension will be referred to as TBC I, and to the second recension as TBC II.

4. TBC I, pp. 57, 176-177.

5. TBC I, p. 57 line 1855.

6. O'Rahilly's translation, TBC I, p. 177, reads "It is not for a woman's body that I have come." It has been noted in

various places that O'Rahilly's translations are often more squeamish and prudish around certain matters, this being a prime example.

7. TBC I, pp. 61, 180; TBC II, pp. 54, 194; Nettlau, p. 66; Ó Béarra, p. 58; O'Rahilly, Stowe, p. 54; Ó Fiannachta, p. 29, simply reports that the events happened as foretold in *Táin Bó Regamna*; Thomas Kinsella (trans.), *The Tain* (Oxford: Oxford University Press, 1969), p. 135; Ciaran Carson (trans.), *The Táin* (New York: Viking, 2007), p. 94.

8. Ernst Windisch (ed.), "Táin bó Regamna," Irische Texte 2.2 (1887), pp. 239-254 at 246-247; Eleanor Hull (ed.), *The Cuchullin Saga in Irish Literature* (London: David Nutt, 1898), p. 106; A. H. Leahy, *Heroic Romances of Ireland, 2 Volumes* (London: David Nutt, 1906), Volume 2, pp. 138-139.

9. John Thomas Koch and John Carey (eds./trans.), *The Celtic Heroic Age: Literary Sources for Ancient Celtic Europe & Early Ireland & Wales* (Aberystwyth and Andover: Celtic Studies Publications, 2003), p. 130.

10. See, for example, TBC I, pp. 19-20, 142-143; TBC II, pp. 25-26, 163.

11. The literature on this is extensive; see Proinsias Mac Cana, "Aspects of the Theme of the King and Goddess in Irish Literature," *Études Celtiques* 7 (1955-1956), pp. 76-114, 356-413; 8 (1958-1959), pp. 59-65.

12. Koch and Carey, pp. 203-208.

13. See Phillip A. Bernhardt-House, "The Intoxicating One: Medb and Celtic Sovereignty Goddesses," *Thorn* 1.3 (Summer 2009), pp. 20-21, for how many female figures who act in the Sovereignty's role are not goddesses, nor euhemerized reflexes of goddesses, even in pre-Christian literature produced by polytheists who have no problems understanding deities' direct interventions in history.

14. Kuno Meyer, "The Wooing of Emer," *Archaeological Review* 1 (1888), pp. 68-75, 150-155, 231-235, 298-307 at 70.

15. Gray, pp. 44-45 §84-85.

16. Gray, pp. 46-51 §93.
17. Tom Peete Cross and Clark Harris Slover (eds.), *Ancient Irish Tales* (London, Bombay, and Sydney: George C. Harrap and Co., Ltd., 1937), p. 329.
18. Koch and Carey, p. 140.
19. For example, TBC I, pp. 30, 152.
20. Hull, pp. 241-242.
21. Koch and Carey, pp. 136-137.
22. Hull, p. 247.
23. Koch and Carey, p. 136.
24. Gray, p. 132.
25. Koch and Carey, p. 52.
26. See William Sayers, "Airdrech, Sirite and Other Early Irish Battlefield Spirits," *Éigse 25* (1991), pp. 45-55.
27. This story exists in many different Greek and Roman sources, and was popular well into the medieval period as well. For a treatment of many of the classical sources, see John Heath, *Actaeon, The Unmannerly Intruder: The Myth and Its Meaning in Classical Literature* (New York: P. Lang, 1992).

Call to the Morrighan
by Frances Billinghurst

Shapeshifting triune daughter of the Great Ernmas
Fading in and out of dreams with bloody desires and lust
Morrigu of the ancient land, whom the Dagda loved
Prophesying heroes and battles that would be lost.

Queen of the Phantoms, chooser of the slain
Stirring blood to a frenzy, Nemain that is her name
The raven of the battlefield with her death defying call
When Badb Catha circles, death will come to all.

Banshee of the shadow realms with terrifying screams
Haunting Irish heroes by appearing in their dreams
King maker, soul destroyer, washer of the ford
Determining the fates of those she chose to die by the sword.

Mistress of the Cauldron, Goddess of sovereignty
Fortune teller, prophetess, maker of all kings
Macha the red-eared heifer, keeper of the land
Bringer of the feminine with her blackthorn rod in hand.

O the mighty Morrighan, the great Phantom Queen
Creating circles of life and death, the seen and the unseen
Shape-shifting hooded crow, the powers of three times three
Protecting all who call to her in their hour of need.

Macha – One Face of the Morrigan
by Morgan Daimler

Macha is a Goddess who appears in several different places in Irish mythology. She is a daughter of Ernmas, sister to Badbh and Anand/Nemain; in mythology these three sisters are the triple Morrighan. *O'Mulconry's Glossary* calls her "machæ .i. badb no asi an tres morrigan", meaning Macha, a scald-crow, or the third Morrigan, (Stokes, 1898). Macha appears as one of the Nemedians, as a Tuatha de Danann, as a "fairy woman," and as a queen. This last one may or may not represent an actual historic queen or a story about the Goddess; the tale itself has many mythic overtones. I tend to favor the view that all the appearances of Macha relate to the Goddess, but that is just my own opinion.

In the first story she appears as the wife of Nemed, of the third race to settle Ireland, and in this tale she "dies," clearing the plains of Ireland for farming. In alternate versions her husband cleared the land and she died there, so he named it for her. In either case, she is linked to the earth and its produce, through her death in exchange for clearing the land for farming. It is also possible that her name "Macha" may mean plain or field (Sjoedstedt, 2000).

She appears in the *Lebor Gabala Erenn* where she is called a daughter of Ernmas. In volume IV of the *Lebor* translation by R. A. S. Macalister, the translator says "Delbaeth ... has three daughters, the famous war-furies Badb, Macha, and Mórrígu, the latter sometimes called Anand or Danand." (Macalister, 1941). In this appearance she is killed in the second battle of Mag Tuired, but Macalister in his introduction to Section VII of the *Lebor Gabala Erenn*, volume IV says that it is logical to believe that this Macha and the Macha of Ard-Macha who curses the men of Ulster are in fact the same deity. At a later point in the text Macalister also posits that Macha was a later addition to the Badb/Anand (Nemain) pairing, saying, "Macha, one of the Badb sisterhood, has a certain individuality of her own, and enjoyed a special cult, probably centered at Armagh (Ard Macha), to which she bequeathed her name. Her intrusion into the Badb sisterhood may be a subsequent development, for the genealogies before us seem to suggest an earlier tradition in which Badb and the variously named third member of the group formed a dyad." (Macalister, 1941). This provides us a variety of interesting information about Macha. We learn that she is the daughter of Delbaeth and Ernmas, and sister to Badb and Anand, one of the three Morrigan. And we learn -- according to the *Lebor Gabala Erenn* anyway -- that Macha falls in battle with Nuada at the hand of Balar of the evil eye. This seems to tell us that she was actually fighting in the battle alongside the other warriors.

All of this information is supported in the "index to persons" of the *Cath Maige Tuired* which references her as one of the Tuatha de Danann, and agrees with the *Lebor Gabala Erenn's* parentage. This index also mentions that in the Banshenchus she is listed as one of the Tuatha de Danann's magic workers, and that in the first battle of Mag Tuired she acts with the other two Morrigan to use magic against the enemy, specifically by sending rain, fog, and showers of blood and fire upon the opposing army. The second battle of Mag Tuired lists the three Morrigan as ban-draoithe, or Druids (Gray, 1983). This tells us that not only is she a warrior, but also a magic user, especially of battle magic.

Next she appears as a fairy woman who marries a farmer named Crunnchu, and becomes pregnant with twins. He goes to a festival held by the king who is bragging of the speed of his horses. Crunnchu, despite being warned by Macha not to speak of her to anyone else, brags that his wife could outrace any horse, and the furious king demands that Crunnchu bring her immediately to race or forfeit his life. Macha begs for a delay as she is in labor, but is denied and forced to race anyway.

She wins, collapsing and birthing her twins just past the finish line and curses the men of Ulster with nine days of labor pain in their greatest hour of need for "nine times nine" generations before dying. To this day the spot carries her name, Emain Macha, where for a long time festivals and assemblies were held, especially at Lughnasah. It is from this story that her associations with horses, childbirth, pregnancy, justice and, again, the produce of the earth -- by marrying a farmer -- are seen. As already mentioned there seems to be a clear connection between this Macha and the Macha of the Tuatha de Danann.

In the final story we see her connection to sexuality, sovereignty, and battle. She is Macha Mog Ruadh, Macha Red-Hair, daughter of one of three kings who share the rulership of Ireland, each ruling for seven years in turn. When her father dies, Macha steps up to rule, but is challenged by the other two kings who do not want to co-rule with a woman. She battles them and wins, and when her seven years are up she refuses to turn leadership over to the others since she is Queen not by blood, but through victory in battle. One of the two kings dies, leaving five sons who would challenge her, so she goes to them in the appearance of a crone or leper and seduces them one by one, tying them up afterwards and thereby defeating them and enslaving them. Finally she marries the last of the original three kings, Cimbaeth. This story has the most tenuous link to the Goddess on the surface, but I have always seen a lot of mythic symbolism in the story. The number of kings and years, as well as Macha going to the five sons disguised as either a crone or leper, and then her marrying the final king to give him full sovereignty, have always struck me more as echoes of the older tales about the goddess of the land choosing the king through trials.

Traditionally the severed heads of enemy warriors were called "Macha's acorn crop," another sign that she was a warrior goddess (Sjoedstedt, 2000). My unverified personal gnosis is that, in each story when she "dies," she is actually just returning to the Otherworld from whence she came, having accomplished what she intended in our world. From a purely personal perspective, I have found her to be fiercely loving and protective of those she calls her own, with a strong "mother" energy to her, but she can be very no-nonsense and unbending as well. She always appears to me as a red-haired warrior woman wearing a cloak of black feathers and riding or walking next to a black or white horse, sometimes both. To me, she is a goddess of the sovereignty of the land, a protector of the weak, and goddess of women and women's issues, especially pregnancy and childbirth -- which is definitely a form of battle.

References:

Gray, E. (1983) *Cath Maige Tuired*. Published by the Irish texts Society.

Macalister, R. (1941). *Lebor Gabala Erenn, volume IV*. Published by the Irish Texts Society.

Sjoestedt, M. (2000) *Celtic Gods and Heroes*. Dover Publications.

Stokes, W. (1898) *O'Mulconry's Glossary*.

An Expansion of Babd's Prophecy from the Second Battle of Mag Tuired
by Judith O'Grady

At the end of the second battle of Mag Tuired, Babd makes a prophecy. Knowing a little about the Ancient Irish poetic rules (last word to first word as well as last line to first line circularity), it is obvious that a number of lines are missing. Here I have filled in those lines with appropriate poetics:

"Peace up to heaven.
Heaven down to earth.
Earth beneath heaven,
Strength in each,
Each in each piled,
Piled like a cup.
A cup very full,
Full of honey;
Mead in abundance.
Abundance flowers,
Flowers like Summer.
Summer in winter. ...
Winter's a blanket,
Blanketing the green.
Green under the wet,
Wet is Summer's peace.
Peace up to heaven ...."

Fulacht na Morrigna
by P. Sufenas Virius Lupus

The Morrígan's Cooking-Pit:
from whence is the name for it?
Not hard to tell, poets say,
though tale was lost in time's fray.

The Hound of Ulster, one night
when fending off Connacht's fight
a wild pig with sling was slain
and stone struck out the pig's brain.

The Hound took pig for boiling
after days-long raid's foiling;
a woman was at hearth's side
who might the meat's fire provide.

"A pig's boiling I would ask —
I have holly spit for task."
"You'll have water, fire, and spit
if you'll sport with me a bit!"

"It's not for sport I stand guard!"
"Then satire you'll hear from bard!"
"Unlawful would satire be
if none of sport comes from me!"

"Then crows will pick at your bones!"
"We all shall lie low as stones,
king, hero, herder alike —
drowned or burned or head on pike."

"If I refuse, what then, Hound?"

"Satire will soon surely sound —
hospitality requires
no harm nor fine beside fires."

"Do you know to whom you speak?"
"With grey wolf's fur or black beak,
red heifer or river's eel
I'd know — deaf or blind — your feel."

"Then have fire and water's boil —
your virtue will not now spoil!"
The Land-Spirit's Queen's deceit
faded into mists' retreat.

Cú Chulainn stood with pig; gone
was shade of the Morrígan…
so with fire and holly spit
he cooked his pig at the pit.

The Hound acted right that night
and from Goddess earned no spite,
thus became the name for it:
the Morrígan's Cooking-Pit.

Badb Catha
by Stephanie Woodfield

I am Victory
I am enchantment
I revel in life, yet I also take it away
I live in the heart that does not fear
I fly over the battlefield draped in the velvet of black feathers,
A battle cry on my blood-stained lips
I dwell in the hearts of the mighty
My law is Conquer or Die

An Morrigan
by Sandy Nickell
Also appeared in Blackbird O'Connell's *A Child's Eye View of Irish Paganism*.

The Crow's Call
by Monika Pleyer

Night is approaching, gentle I hear her
clad in velvet she comes,
a crow her envoy
she has spent the high summer
at the ford, washing,
washing,
'til the flow of the waters turned crimson
and brown

give me my gown you have washed
by the waters
give it to me, I will wear it with pride
old battle crow, you have chosen wisely
let me lead your name, ancient one,
in this fight

cool is the Night, after long hours of battle,
the crow's soft cries mingle
with prayers of my own
tonight, it is me she wants,
me she asks for
the dark queen of phantoms
will take me home

Valkyrie Queen
by Sara Star

The Morrigan, Allecto, and Lamia: Irish Deities and Interpretatio Hibernica of Classical Myth
by P. Sufenas Virius Lupus

The Morrígan is known best from two medieval Irish tales: *Cath Maige Tuired*, which dates from the ninth century CE, but exists in a twelfth-century recension in a sixteenth-century manuscript;[1] and *Táin Bó Cúailnge*, which dates in its earliest portions to the seventh century CE, but which exists in four recensions, of which the oldest is in the late-eleventh/early-twelfth-century manuscript Lebor na hUidre.[2] It has generally been agreed since the late nineteenth century, however, that an inscription to the Gaulish goddess [C]athobodua might be an earlier analogue to the Irish goddess, since the latter is sometimes called *Badb Catha*, "raven of battle," which is a direct Irish cognate to the Gaulish theonym.[3] The difficulty with this interpretation, of course, is that the original inscription is missing the first letter; and, direct mythological or cultic cognates between ancient Gaulish (a polytheistic culture and a P-Celtic language) and medieval Irish (a Christian culture and a Q-Celtic language) are notoriously controversial and difficult to definitively prove.

What other traces of a Morrígan-like deity might exist in earlier Irish, or other Insular Celtic cultures, however, is a question that has not been explored very much. Further, what interpretations of Morrígan actually exist within medieval Irish texts, which link her to other goddesses and divine female figures from the classical world, has also not received very much attention.[4] The present discussion will be devoted to exploring the evidence for the Morrígan's connection to two different classical goddesses, Allecto (one of the Furies recognized by Roman tradition), and Lamia (the name of a variety of female monsters, witches, and minor divine figures).

What will hopefully emerge from this exploration is evidence not only for the possible existence of the Morrígan or a group of Morrígan-like beings in older Insular Celtic sources, but also the ways in which the medieval Irish also understood the Morrígan as a goddess equal in fierceness and fame to the older Graeco-Roman goddesses.

Allecto

One particular reference in the first recension of the Ulster Cycle epic *Táin Bó Cúailnge* has drawn a great deal of attention and speculation on its significance for understanding a medieval Irish author's classical knowledge and the influence of classical models on Irish literature,[5] and yet little attention has been paid to the content and significance of the reference itself in its context. This is the mention of the classical Fury Allecto in relation to the Morrígan.

> *Céin bátár didiu in tslóig oc tochim Maige Breg, forrumai Allechtu colléic, noch is í Mórrígan són I ndeilb eúin co mboí forsin chorthi hi Temair Cúailngi.*[6]

While the army was going over Mag mBreg Allecto came for a while, that is, the Mórrígan, in the form of a bird which perched on the pillar-stone in Temair Cúailnge.[7]

This is a classic case of *Interpretatio Hibernica*,[8] because the initiative for the comparison is coming from an Irish author, writing in Irish, in relation to an Irish figure. In this particular case the classical figure seems to have precedence since she is named first.

Allecto was a figure known elsewhere in Irish glosses, including an extended Latin gloss on a passage from the *Liber Hymnorum*'s version of *Amra Choluim Chille*,[9] which presents a rather unique interpretation of classical literature in itself.

> *Tres filiae Orci quae uocantur diuersis nominibus in caelo et in terra et in inferno; in caelo quidem Stenna et Euriale et Medusa; .i. Clothus Lacessis Antropus; in inferno Electo Migera Stifone.*[10]

> The three daughers of Orcus, which were called by diverse names in heaven and on the earth and in hell; indeed in heaven (they were) Stheno and Euryale and Medusa; that is (on earth) Clotho, Lachesis, Atropos; in hell Allecto, Megaera and Tisiphone.[11]

This interpretation links the three Gorgons (daughters of Phorcys, who was interpreted as "Porcus" in Irish and then linked to Orcus), the three Fates, and the three Furies to a common ancestry, though the latter two are not related to either Orcus or Phorcys in any attested source. A more vivid or creative demonstration of the learned medieval Irish familiarity and flexibility with re-envisioning classical myth could not be imagined! These varying groups of three fateful and/or frightful female deities would certainly seem to be comparable to the Morrígan in some sense, since she is often one of three such aggressive supernatural female figures in Irish narrative. But a closer look at Virgil's *Aeneid*, a text with which the Irish (and all medieval Christian cultures) were most familiar, might bear further insights into why such a comparison would have been made.

In Virgil's *Aeneid*, Book Seven, we find Allecto, under Juno's orders, stirring up trouble between the forces of Aeneas and the Trojans, and King Latinus and his people. When

Allecto is first summoned, she is described as being able to assume many forms,[12] which fits the Morrígan's ability to assume a variety of both human and animal forms in the *Táin*. In particular, the Morrígan assumes the form of an eel to hinder Cú Chulainn's fighting ability in the ford against Loch.[13] This is similar to Allecto's arousal of a Bacchic-like fury in Queen Amata by throwing one of the snakes from her hair to poison her with resentment.[14] In her incitement of Turnus against the Trojans, Allecto initially assumes the form of an old woman, before revealing herself in her full furious appearance.[15] Likewise, the Morrígan also assumes the form of an old woman in order to trick Cú Chulainn into healing her by blessing her for each of the wounds he inflicted on her when she opposed him in the ford.[16]

While there is not a direct one-to-one correspondence between Allecto and the Morrígan in all aspects, nor a complete parallel in the plot-lines and motives behind their actions in each narrative, the similarity of both figures in being able to assume many forms — among them an elderly woman and a serpent or eel — and being part of a triplicity of divine female figures demonstrates that, if nothing else, the Irish literati were adept at noting what we might now term comparative mythological details in the two literatures. It is also to be noted that the Irish version of the *Aeneid*, known as the *Imtheachta Aeniasa*, "The Journeying of Aeneas," has a scene that is very close to the original Latin version in which Allecto does the same incitements of various enmities against Aeneas due to Juno's resentment of the hero.[17] It was, thus, a scene familiar to most literate audiences in medieval Ireland, which would have been the primary readers of the *Táin Bó Cúailnge* in the forms currently known to exist.

Lamia

What is particularly fascinating about the Morrígan in cases of *Interpretatio Hibernica* is that she is not only "interpreted by" classical figures in narratives concerning her, as with Allecto, but she also is used "to interpret" classical and other figures in Irish commentaries on and translations of non-Irish sources. The ninth-century Irish scholar in Carolingian France, Joannes Scottus Eriugena, glossed a Latin Vulgate biblical manuscript of Isaiah 34:14 (*ibi cubauit lamia et inuenit sibi requiem*) as follows:

Lamia monstrum in feminae figura .i. morrígain.

Lamia: a monster in feminine form, that is, the Morrígan.[18]

"Lamia" can refer to any of several possible female figures in Greek and Roman mythology.[19] Interestingly, Jerome's own glosses on the *lamia* include the Hebrew Lilith, as well as the Greek Erinyes and the Latin Furies (of whom Allecto was one). Here, however, Eriugena has instead inserted something which was familiar to him from Irish mythology, and would no doubt have been recognized by his students who may have been using one of the three manuscripts which contained this gloss. Further, as discussed by Máire Herbert,[20] the word *morrígan* is used in the sense of "witch" or "demon" to refer to Jocasta the mother of Oedipus in the Irish version of Statius' *Thebaid*, *Togail na Tebe*.[21] This agrees with the more general usage of the Morrígan's name to refer to various types of malignant spirits and creatures in the tenth-century Irish glossary *Sanas Cormaic*.[22] In a syllogistic manner, it would appear that the glossing of *lamia* with the Morrígan (or, perhaps more appropriately in this context, "*a* morrígan"), the explanation of the Morrígan via Allecto, and (via Jerome) the connection of the Furies/Erinyes and Lilith to *lamiae* can be taken as something of an established fact for the Irish monastic scholars.

Lamiae appear elsewhere in early Irish sources. In an ecclesiastical text attributed to the bishops Patricius, Auxilius and Isernius, which may therefore date to the mid-fifth century, *The First Synod of St. Patrick*, the following statement occurs:

> *Christianus qui crediderit esse lamiam in saeculo, quae interpraetatur striga, anathemazandus.*
>
> A Christian who believes that there is such a thing in the world as a vampire, that is to say, a witch, is to be anathematized.[23]

If this document does indeed date to the mid-fifth century, when Irish paganism was still a major influence on the larger society, such a worry on the part of the evangelizing Christians is understandable. But is it possible that in this worry, there might in fact be some connection to belief in a pre-Christian female deity of some sort, in accordance with the understanding of *lamiae* given by Jerome, but in the specifically Irish context—in other words, *morrígna* generally, or the Morrígan herself, perhaps?

While we do not have any evidence from Ireland which can shed light on this with certainty, we do have some interesting evidence from Roman Britain in the second to fourth centuries. On an altar from the fort of Condercum (modern Benwell) on the eastern end of Hadrian's Wall near Newcastle-upon-Tyne, an inscription occurs in dedication to the Three *Lamiae*, *LAMIIS TRIBVS*.[24] From the same site, there is also a dedication to the Three Mother Goddesses of the Parade-Ground.[25] While one cannot assume that all triads of female figures are reducible to one goddess or sets of goddesses in triplicate, the coincidence of both the Three Lamiae and the Three Mother Goddesses of the Parade Ground at this site is suggestive, not least because the Morrígan has her fierce and witch-like aspects, but she is also a warrior in addition to being a goddess connected to motherhood[26] and thus would be a particularly appropriate goddess to be a patroness of the warrior-activities which would occur on the parade grounds of the fort at Condercum. It seems possible, though by no means certain, that through this chain of equivalences in *Interpretatio Hibernica*, perhaps some pre-Christian belief in a triple-aspected, fierce warrior-mother goddess could be conjectured to have been recognized in the religions of the wider Insular Celtic realm.

We have examined two cases of *Interpretatio Hibernica* — the attempt to understand and interpret the practices of the pagan Irish through the lenses and filters of the classically literate Christian Irish — in relation to the Morrígan. These were done, perhaps, with some knowledge of pieces of pagan belief and practice, but on other occasions (and potentially these ones as well) with no basis other than the earlier interpretations and writings of their own *Interpretatio Hibernica*-employing literary forbearers, as well as the comparative interests of Christians like Jerome as their paradigm. Sometimes this variety of exploration might yield valuable insights into the actual nature of pre-Christian practices, while at other points a classical and Christian bibliographic literary itinerary will be the only result; but both of these possibilities are of great utility. One could potentially take a broad view on these matters, and therefore consider every piece of medieval Irish literature that purports to give an account of the beliefs and practices of the pagan Irish to be in the mode of *Interpretatio Hibernica*, which would force one to question every such occurrence and every piece of information which has thus far been marshaled for the purposes of the reconstruction of pre-Christian Irish, and more widely Celtic, religions.

However, an equally valid option might be to adopt a more narrow view, and to employ the paradigm of *Interpretatio Hibernica* in those cases where there does not seem to be precedent elsewhere in the Irish literary tradition, nor in Celtic and Indo-European comparative contexts, for the associations and connections which a particular text suggests. Both options are certainly useful, and there is truth in each of the broad and narrow applications of the paradigm. But, as ever, it would appear that the best course would be to navigate somewhere down the middle, between Péist Chonchinn (i.e. Scylla) and Coire Breccáin (i.e. Charybdis), as it were.

In the case of the Morrígan, we have both modes occurring, it seems: just as the Morrígan gets interpreted by the comparison with Allecto from the Latin epic of Virgil's *Aeneid* in the first recension of the Irish epic *Táin Bó Cúailnge*, the Morrígan (or, perhaps more accurately, the *morrígna* as a class of female spiritual beings) in turn is used to interpret *lamiae* and *lilitu*, and may in fact point toward the existence of such beings in other Insular Celtic contexts, whether as one variety of spiritual being, or as a specific triad of goddesses. As worthy a recipient for modern devotions as the Morrígan and her colleagues are, they are likewise potentially powerful figures as keys for the interpretation of the Irish tradition, and for potential connections through syncretism to other polytheistic traditions that are likewise being revived in the modern world.

Notes

1. Elizabeth Gray (ed./trans.), *Cath Maige Tuired: The Second Battle of Mag Tuired*, Irish Texts Society Vol. 52 (Dublin and London: Irish Texts Society, 1982).

2. The Morrígan only appears in the first three recensions of TBC, and the fourth recension does not currently exist in an edited form. Recension I: Cecile O'Rahilly (ed./trans.), *Táin Bó Cúailnge, Recension I* (Dublin: Dublin Institute for Advanced Studies, 1967). Recension II: Cecile O'Rahilly (ed./trans.), *Táin Bó Cualnge from the Book of Leinster* (Dublin: Dublin Institute for Advanced Studies, 1968); Cecile O'Rahilly (ed.), *The Stowe Version of Táin Bó Cuailnge* (Dublin: Dublin Institute for Advanced Studies, 1978).. Recension III: Max Nettlau (ed.), "The Fragment of the Táin Bó Cúailnge in MS. Egerton 93 (ff. 26a 1-35b 2)," Revue Celtique 15 (1894), 62-78, 198-208; Pádraig Ó Fiannachta (ed.), *Táin Bó Cuailnge The Maynooth Manuscript* (Dublin: Dublin Institute for Advanced Studies, 1980); Feargal Ó Béarra (trans.), "Táin Bó Cuailnge: Recension III," Emania 15 (1996), pp. 47-65. Further reference to O'Rahilly's edition/translation of the first recension, relevant to the discussion to follow, will be referred to as TBC I.

3. William M. Hennessy, "The Ancient Irish Goddess of War," Revue Celtique 1 (1870), pp. 32-55; Proinsias Mac Cana, "Celtic Goddesses of Sovereignty," in Elisabeth Benard and Beverly Moon (eds.), *Goddesses Who Rule* (Oxford: Oxford University Press, 2000), pp. 85-99 at 91.

4. The only major exception is Phillip A. Bernhardt-House, "Interpretatio Hibernica," Eolas: *Journal of the American Society of Irish Medieval Studies* 2 (2007), pp. 45-60.

5. Rudolf Thurneysen, *Die irische Helden- und Königsage bis zum 17. Jahrhundert* (Halle: Max Niemeyer, 1921), p. 96; Gerard Murphy, "Studies in Irish Literature and History, by James Carney" (review), *Éigse* 8 (1956), pp. 152-164 at 157-158

note 4; Rijcklof Hofman, "Some New Facts Concerning the Knowledge of Vergil in Early Medieval Ireland," *Études Celtiques* 25 (1988), pp. 189-212 at 197; Ruairí Ó hUiginn, "The Background and Development of Táin Bó Cúailnge,' in J. P. Mallory (ed.), *Aspects of the Táin* (Belfast: December Publications, 1992), pp. 29-67 at 40; Varese Layzer, *Signs of Weakness: Juxtaposing Irish Tales and the Bible* (Sheffield: Sheffield Academic Press, 2001), pp. 27, 67-68.

6. TBC I, p. 30 lines 954-956.

7. TBC I, p. 152.

8. Bernhardt-House, p. 48: "Understanding the multivalent medieval usages and understandings of the word interpretatio, and especially conscious of both the utility as well as the biases present in using information from sources exhibiting the Interpretatio Romana in examining Celtic religion, I would like to suggest that envisioning these Irish glosses and connections is neither mere learned fancy nor simply an indicator of the early Irish literary curriculum, but that they are instead what I would like to term Interpretatio Hibernica." Recall that *Interpretatio Romana* is the phrase, first used by Tacitus in Germania 43, which reflects the tendency of Roman authors to compare foreign deities to their own, and which gets used by modern scholars to reflect syncretistic linking of deities in inscriptions (e.g. Apollo Belenus, Mars Teutates, Sulis Minerva, etc.). On a more nuanced understanding of these types of syncretism, see P. Sufenas Virius Lupus, *A Serpent Path Primer* (Anacortes: The Red Lotus Library, 2012), pp. 8-11.

9. The *Liber Hymnorum* is a late-eleventh/early-twelfth-century manuscript; the *Amra Choluim Chille* is a seventh-century poem lamenting the death of St. Colum Cille/Columba, the famous Irish saint, poet, and scholar who founded the monastery of Iona in the Hebrides, which became a major center of scholarship for Ireland and Britain, and was the jumping-off point for missions into Scotland and northern Britain.

10. J.H. Bernard and R. Atkinson (eds./trans.), *The Irish Liber Hymnorum*, 2 Volumes (London: Henry Bradshaw Society, 1898), Vol. 1, p. 164.

11. W.B. Stanford, "Monsters and Odyssean Echoes in the Early Hiberno-Latin and Irish Hymns," in John J. O'Meara and Bernd Naumann (eds.), *Latin Script and Letters, A.D. 400-900: Festschrift presented to Ludwig Bieler on the occasion of his 70th Birthday* (Leiden: E. J. Brill, 1976), pp. 113-117 at 114.

12. H. Rushton Fairclough (ed./trans.), *Virgil*, 2 Volumes (Cambridge: Harvard University Press, 1918), Vol. 2, pp. 24-25 line 328.

13. TBC I, pp. 61, 176-177, 180.

14. Fairclough, Vol. 2, pp. 26-31.

15. Fairclough, Vol. 2, pp. 32-35.

16. TBC I, pp. 62-63, 181-182.

17. George Calder (ed./trans.), *Imtheachta Aeniasa: The Irish Aeneid*, introduced by Erich Poppe, *Irish Texts Society Vol. 6* (London and Dublin: Irish Texts Society, 1995), pp. 102-111.

18. Whitley Stokes and John Strachan (eds./trans.), Thesaurus Paleohibernicus, 2 Volumes (Dublin: Dublin Institute for Advanced Studies, 1975), Vol 1, p. 2; John J. Contreni and Pádraig P. Ó Néill (eds./trans.). *Glossae divinae historiae: The Biblical Glosses of John Scottus Eriugena* (Florence: Sismel/Edizioni del galluzzo, 1997), p. 146 §298. John Shaw, "Indo-European Dragon-Slayers and Healers, and the Irish Account of Dian Cécht and Méiche," *Journal of Indo-European Studies* 34.1/2 (2006), pp. 153-181 at 164-165, incorrectly states that Morrígan was glossed by lamia, rather than Morrígan glossing lamia.

19. Carl Kerényi, *The Gods of the Greeks* (London and New York: Thames & Hudson, Inc., 1980), pp. 38-40.

20. Máire Herbert, "Transmutations of an Irish Goddess," in Sandra Billington and Miranda Green (eds.), *The Concept of the Goddess* (London: Routledge, 1996), pp. 141-151 at 148.

21. George Calder (ed./trans.), *Togail na Tebe: The Thebaid of Statius* (Cambridge: Cambridge University Press, 1922), pp. 6-7 lines 87-88.

22. Kuno Meyer (ed.), *Sanas Cormaic (Cormac's Glossary)*, compiled by Cormac Úa Cuillenáin, King-Bishop of Cashel in the Tenth Century (Felinfach: Llanerch Publishers, 1994), p. 58 §697.

23. Ludwig Bieler (ed./trans.), *The Irish Penitentials, Scriptores Latini Hiberniae 5* (Dublin: Dublin Institute for Advanced Studies, 1975), pp. 56-57 §16.

24. R. G. Collingwood and R. P. Wright (eds.), *The Roman Inscriptions of Britain I: Inscriptions on Stone*, addenda/corrigenda by R. S. O. Tomlin (Stroud: Alan Sutton Publishing Limited, 1995), pp. 440-441 §1331.

25. Collingwood and Wright, p. 441 §1334.

26. Herbert, p. 143; Shaw pp. 166-167

The Washer at the Ford
by Jennifer Lawrence

Raven queen,
Scarlet-eyed,
Hands full of bloody laundry,
You sit at the river's edge.
Patient,
For so many men come to you
in their time.
Battle-bright,
Sword-steel wingspan,
And the cruel scything grip
of your talons.
Boldly,
You stride amongst the wounded.
Boldly,
You dine on death.
Boldly,
You winnow weak and strong alike.
Cuchulain's bane,
Terror of the night,
Dark Lady,
Who is there who can stand in your way,
And end the ringing clash of steel,
Silence the screams of the maimed,
And wash away the blood?

Letter to the Morrigan
(the kind She always feels is long overdue)
by Xochiquetzal Duti Odinsdottir

Ma'am,

I finished another job again. I really don't know why I keep getting these tickets. I journey to places and do weird things there. Yet, when I come home and crawl between my sheets, feeling the stiffness in my joints, I can't help but smile.

Sometimes, I have to wonder, why? What the fuck? Why can't someone else do it? I've gone three times this week. Send another of Yours, would you? I'm fucking tired!

You listen, sitting quiet and preternaturally calm, gazing, gauging. Your cold and calculated gaze reminding me that this tirade of mine is a rarity You let me indulge in, especially in front of You. Sometimes, I wonder if You get a secret kick out of watching me stomp around and shouting my indignation. You always know when to cut me off and send me off to do the very thing I didn't want to do. You have so many other people, who do what I do, but not the way I do.

I have been in this relationship with You (General/Soldier? Handler/Spook? What exactly do we call it, Ma'am?) quite a few years now. I'm older, wizened, and much more cautious than I used to be. When we first met, You were the Spiritual Director and I wanted in. My Dedication, changed that a tiny bit, I think .... When it became clear that You weren't prepared (which to this day, still catches me by surprise to discuss) for what I was bringing to the table (not just me, but my work with my Ancestors and the PreColumbian pantheons of the Aztec, Inca, and Maya, not to mention the histories of the smaller sects in that entire landmass), was that when I first garnered Your attention? Was that when You first became interested in what I was seeing behind my dark eyes?

These are all questions I ask myself as I get ready to do another journey, to explore some other land on Your business, or request, or whim.

You and I have gone down some interesting roads. Yet, of all the deities I am ordained to, You have not asked for blood to be spilled for You, You've not asked me to take anyone to my bed for You. The only assignments I get from You are to go and gather facts and information. Only after careful weighing of every avenue do I receive orders to march into a fight. I rarely know what the fight is actually about (does any soldier ever really know?), but that doesn't matter to me. My choices were mine to make, just as the day I ordained and You asked if I was sure, if I wanted this working relationship with You to be cemented. My vows weren't taken lightly, Ma'am. I stand by them to this day.

You have never asked me to be blind, you have never asked me to just be obedient. You expect me to have a mouth (a rather brash and crass one at that) and You expect me to use it. You expect me to look at certain orders and go striding into Your space and demand to understand, to see the picture from your viewpoint. You don't expect blind obeisance from me, and that's good. I work well in our structure; our dynamic is suited for the both of us, I think. You get to know where my boundaries are, and how they can broaden (sometimes without my being aware of it) to suit Your needs. Because at the end, even if I disagree with the order, I recognize that it's not for me to understand, but for You. You get where it's going, I just get to nudge things to work out the way You need them to.

So, here I am, preparing myself, doing the breathing and trance techniques I've honed and worked on for years before turning pagan (and considering my Catholic upbringing, rogue would also be apt) and getting ready for another task.

As I look back on the service I have provided, I am gladdened that I have been able to perform my duties as well and decorously as I have. You, of all people, know that my mouth gets me into enough trouble, but, when I go out, in Your name, bearing Your mark, doing Your work, I do so with pride in being chosen, and with the understanding that You know I will not fail you, even if the odds appear stacked against me. You know that I will find a way to succeed. It may not be pretty, but dammit, I get You results.

So, what are my next orders, Ma'am?

Dutifully,

XDO

PS That mess, in the Fae court, totally wasn't my fault. But then, You didn't say I had to go in clean and stay that way. You just said to go in clean, get it done, and get out. Sorry. But, these things happen.

How I Met the Morrigan
Or, A Series of Unfortunate Events, Only Most of Which are My Fault
by Hannah Lipsky

People often ask me how to find a patron god or goddess. I tell them they're asking the wrong person, because they really don't want to do it my way. And then I tell them this story. Sometimes I start by showing them the pendant I around my neck with a crow on the front and the summary of the story on the back. It reads, "Everyone saw this coming but me."

When I first moved to California, I was not a pagan. I was something like a polytheistic agnostic: there is no god, but there might be many. I also lived about ten minutes away from the venue for PantheaCon, which is how this whole thing started.

My pagan friends were going to the convention and I offered to let them stay at my place. They accepted, and invited me to go with them.

"No thanks," I told them. "I'm not a pagan, remember? But enjoy Super Happy Pagan Fun Time. We can hang out when you get back."

The first day of PantheaCon arrived, and things went as planned. My friends went to the convention, then we all got dinner together and generally had a good time. They once more invited me to come with them to the convention, and I once more told them no. The second day went similarly, Sunday looked as if it were going to follow the same pattern. I woke up and chatted with my friends as they prepared to leave. I was invited a third time, and for a third time I declined. My plan was to go back to sleep as soon as everyone was gone.

My friends left. I got back in bed. That's when things stopped going according to plan. (They still haven't started again.)

I'm very good at ignoring my intuition. But every once in a great while, I will feel a call so strong that even I can't ignore it. I hadn't been in bed for more than ten minutes when suddenly I knew that I had to go to PantheaCon. I didn't know why. But I couldn't picture my day unfolding in any other way.

I got out of bed and threw on some Renaissance Faire garb, because hey, pagans are into that, right? I hopped on the light rail and headed down to the convention. On my walk to the hotel, I passed some people in cloaks. That's how I knew I was headed in the right direction.

My friends found me, and were perplexed, but happy that I was there. They showed me a program guide. Some of the lectures looked interesting; some looked like things I was already familiar with from my background in classics. Some of the rituals looked silly, some seemed cool, and one immediately stood out to me as an absolutely terrible idea.

"Someone here is doing a Morrigan ritual? Why on earth would you do that? Who says to themselves, 'What my life really needs right now is more chaos and violence!' Who would go to a thing like that?"

I may not have been a pagan, but I have been a mythology geek all my life. I knew exactly who the Morrigan was. Well, perhaps not exactly.

After a few more minutes venting my disbelief that anyone would attend such a ritual I found a couple of lectures that sounded good, and off we all went to our respective lectures and rituals and workshops. One friend of mine was undecided. I dragged her along to a storytelling workshop that sounded interesting. It was not.

After dinner was another storytelling talk, and I was convinced that this one would be worth it. It sounded perfect, assuredly far better than the previous one.

It was not. While the previous workshop was mediocre, this one was absolutely terrible. Think about the worst freshman English course you took in college. Now imagine two solid hours of that, while your friend alternates between trying to fall asleep in her chair, rolling her eyes at the lecturer, and sending you death glares for getting her into this.

Afterwards, I apologized to my friend. I'd wasted two time slots worth of her limited PantheaCon time with my poor choices. Obviously I was striking out today and shouldn't be allowed to make my own decisions. There was only one suitable act of contrition – I waived my right to make decisions for the rest of the night. Wherever she chose to go to next, I would go.

Those of you with a keen sense of dramatic irony can guess what was in the next time slot.

There were at least fifty people in line for the Morrigan ritual when we got there, and over a hundred more showed up in the next few minutes. When I read about the ritual in the program, the names next to it – T. Thorn Coyle and Morpheus Ravenna – meant nothing to me. The rest of PantheaCon did not share my ignorance, and now it seemed that most of the convention was here in line, waiting to see what kind of ritual the two well-known priestesses had created.

My friend was beginning to think this might be a mistake. I assured her that yes, this was a mistake. Can we leave now?

No. She stayed, and so I had to stay as well. I don't go back on my word once given.

Once more, I had a plan. I decided I was going to sit quietly in the corner of the room and do my best not to draw anything's attention. My logic went as follows: I don't know if any of these things exist, but if they do, then the Morrigan is very scary and I don't want her in my life.

We walked into the room. It was dark. There were things painted on banners on the walls. There were people drumming and chanting, and everyone involved was wearing elaborate costumes. Red and black and ravens everywhere. This was my first ever public ritual – as far as I knew, this was just how things were. It was all appropriately scary. I found a chair in the far corner and sat down. So far, so good.

Not so good. No sooner had I sat down then Thorn told everyone to stack the chairs in the corners and come stand in the center of the room.

I revised the plan to "stand quietly near the center of the room and try not to draw anything's attention." That still sounded fairly safe.

Thorn began talking about the ritual, and specifically, mentioned that at the end of it people would have the opportunity to take an oath on the Sword of the Morrigan.

It was at this point that I discovered I had a new personal bar for absolutely terrible ideas.

Making promises is not a safe thing – one got me into this, after all. Making promises to gods is even less safe. Making promises to terrifying goddesses who revel in bloodshed and really don't like to be disappointed? Once again, I found myself asking who would do such a thing. I came to the conclusion that everyone else in the room was completely insane. I am still not entirely sure I was wrong, except about the "else" part.

Then the internal discussion of terrible ideas ceased and the grounding and centering started. This was something I was vaguely familiar with, and it seemed safe enough. I'd been in the room for ten whole minutes at this point, and nothing had tried to eat me yet.

The invocation involved a lot more screaming than I'd expected, but again, this was my first public ritual; I thought maybe that's just how these things go. No one else appeared worried. When the guided meditation began, I decided to follow along. It was better than standing alone with my thoughts in a crowded dark room for an hour and a half. What was the worst that could happen?

Everything went fine at first. Everything always goes fine, at first.

And then Thorn started talking about fear. She said, of the fear, "So weak. So human."

Now that I know more about Thorn, I know she meant no insult. But at the time, I felt insulted. I felt as if humans were being insulted. Most of my best friends are human, and I don't typically stand for anyone insulting them in my presence.

And that's when I said, very clearly and intentionally in my head, the words that will probably end up engraved on my tombstone.

"Bring it on, bitch."

And that's when it began to feel like there was someone else there.

I have yet to successfully explain why challenging the Morrigan seemed like a good idea. I don't regret it, but I also don't recommend it as a general practice. I have tried to be more temperate in my language towards her ever since. Mostly.

But at the moment, I was in no mood to be temperate. I wanted her out of my head. I explained that I was trying very, very hard to remove the violence and chaos from my life and my personality. Her influence was the least helpful possible thing for that goal. She had nothing I wanted.

The Morrigan disagreed. I argued. She told me to look closer. And finally, we found something to agree on. The warrior as protector. I didn't know, then, that this is as much who she is as her better known, more blood-soaked aspects. I just knew that it was something that was a part of both of us.

I don't know how long this conversation took, but when I was aware of the outside world once more, there was some chanting and dancing, which I quite enjoyed, and some shouting, which I found excessive. By this time I had quite forgotten what Thorn had said would happen at the end of the ritual.

As soon as the sword came out, I remembered. And instantly, the oath was there, in my head, ready. I knew what I had to swear.

But there were too many of us to take the oaths all at once, and so they were taken in four quarters. I was in the last. I stepped back, argued with myself, asked myself if this was really what I wanted. And the answer came back, yes. It was a simple oath, and yet far more complicated than it seemed at the time. I simply swore to protect. Little did I know how far those two small words would take me.

Advice
by Jennifer Lawrence

Just because the Phantom Queen's hand may be
gloved in blood past the elbow
Doesn't mean you shouldn't shake it, if she offers;
She's the honest sort, brutally so,
With no need for deceptions or lies.
Whether you draw back your hand whole and unscathed
or a gory stump,
The fingers (when you find them)
Will still bear all the rings they did before you met her
(And anyway, it's rude to refuse,
and you know how much value their kind puts on good
 manners);
Though she might bear many roles --
 -- warrior, prophet, bestower of kingship --
go by more than one name (or shape),
Still, she's not two-faced;
The honesty in those red, red eyes might kill,
But the blade will end up in your heart,
not buried in your back.
Don't scorn her greeting, if it comes, or her aid;
Cuchulainn did that thrice,
and look at how that ended for him.
You are no Lugh's son, no legend,
and however much pride you might have for yourself,
It isn't wise to piss off a goddess
who already knows how you will die
before she's ever met you.
Don't give her a reason to wash your clothes in the stream;
Instead, speak plainly and kindly,
Tell no lies,
offer no insults or bargains,

never beg,
and you might walk away from the meeting
with both your eyes still in their sockets.
Ay, now that's a story to tell your grandchildren,
should you live long enough to have any.

Shieldmaiden's Song
by Morpheus Ravenna

Storm front walks the landscape,
Hooded dark in thunderhead, towering,
Massed weight of storm cascading from shoulders,
Sweeping down to cloak the shadowed land in sheets of rain,
Whispering mist trails behind.
In your wake the dead rise
In the mist the dead rise

Tree tips bare rake the sky
Sharp spear-points glinting wet in the dawn,
A forest of spears, shuddering in the spirit wind,
Ravening for battle,
Massing before you.
Over the spear-points the black wings thunder
Over the spear-points you are winging
Reveling in storm and terror,
Raven-folk gathering,
Tribes of your nation,
We come to you
We rise to you

Phantom Queen, your hollow eyes pour nightmare
And the deep and endless hunger of the grave.
Kind folk turn from you in awe,
Good folk, hoping never to hear you speak their names.
But I have heard you.
I have heard the haunting cry of your voice
And I cannot unhear it.
I have heard the cry of destiny,
I have heard the war drum thundering.
In the night beating

In my chest beating
And I will open for you
I will open for you the Gate
I will give you this life

No other dawn is coming but this one that has come,
The day of calling,
The day in which we live.
And I in my small frame, breathing courage,
No great chieftain I, but all I am is given.
I will heed the war drum
I will heed your calling
O Queen of mine, terrible in your beauty,
Make of me an ardent spear
Lifted by the strong heart of a hero.
I am yours utterly
I am your weapon,
I am yours utterly
I am your shieldmaiden

In the blood light of dawn
Sky wet with cast droplets, singing blood,
Silence before thunder, harrowing,
Comes the storm Queen,
Comes the great Queen,
Morrigan cloaked in the red dawn
Destiny cloaked in the red dawn.

Raven
by Morgaine Nightshade

The Morrigan's Charge
by Morgaine Nightshade

In the depths of your pain, your strength and courage arise
Beyond the panic and anxiety,

I am there
To encourage you, to help you, to strengthen you

Trust in me
I am taking care of you, in dark times and light.

Trust in yourself. Your spirit is limitless.

You have only two choices.

You can give up. The pain and misery will consume you.
You lay yourself to die.
Or, you get up, keep on moving, fighting: exercise no matter how much it hurts,
You keep on doing what you know is necessary. Keep your dreams alive.
Experience new things.
Do often what inspires and excites you. Discover the unknown.

I am the inspiration
I am the flow of all things
I am the creative spark of life.

I Am
by Morgaine Nightshade

I am mistress of magic
Lady of the elements
Goddess of the moon of Avalon and the settling sun,

I am in everything that is was and will be.
I am the chalice filled with grace.
I am the portal through which all things must pass in their own
    time.
I am the cauldron of rebirth and transformation.
I am the devourer and the life giver.

I winter the dark periods of your life.
Be strong. Have faith.
Without the winter there will be no spring.
I am the spirit within that will never die.

I am the challenger.
I challenge you to face your fears, move beyond your illness.
I challenge you to take my hands and follow me.
I show you your faults, your failures, so that you shall
    overcome them.

I am in your nightmares but I don't create them.
I am the fear that shackles
I am that which makes you lose control.
I am the strength that comes after enduring battles.
I show you the demons in your own mind.

The Mother's Words
by Morgaine Nightshade

I will never give you more then you can bear.
The way to get true power, strength and confidence isn't easy
    for anyone.
The way to harmony and health in mind, body, and soul comes
through harsh lessons.

Live your passion.
Be passionate in all that you do
Feel the fiery energy and rejoice.
Allow yourself to be happy.
Enjoy the little things.

Negative thought forms easily create more anxiety;
clean center and ground yourself.
Banish negative energies within and around you.
Frustration and anger can be your downfall if not used
    correctly.

Be strong and proud,
courageous and kind;
you are much stronger and wiser than you think you are.

Lean on me, surrender with all your dreams, hopes, as well as
    your fears and failures.
I will take your hand and transform you,
lead you to your life's purpose.

When you fall,
when you feel that your last time has come,
when you feel that it is over,
that you can't go on;

When you feel that you have hit the rock bottom,

I am there giving you strength to continue:
breathing new life into your veins.

When you feel that the madness has won,
That you are beyond hysteria,
That there is no turning back,
No way of a normal life,
I am there.

When you feel so alone and empty,
That nothing helps to ease the pain,
Come to me,
I will be there to hold you.

Don't let anyone belittle you,
don't let anyone oppress you,
don't let anyone harass you.

Learn to love yourself as I love you.

Call on me and I will be there.
I will guide you.

I have shielded you, I have challenged you,
You fight no battle alone.

When The Morrigan Calls...
by Blackbird O'Connell

It has been so long, it is hard for me to even think back to when I first realized that someone was calling me to this faith. Back when I first found paganism in 1999 and I had just begun studying Wicca (which was only the first six or so months of my journey) within the first few months of my practicing She revealed herself to me -- long flowing, but tousled black hair to the middle of Her back, wearing what appeared to be an all black body suit, and both Her hair and body were adorned with unorganized black feathers. She stood strong and tall, clad with a short sword in scabbard. She didn't speak at the time. She just stared at me as I did Her. Then, as quick as She came, She was gone. That moment sent me on a rampage of research.

It didn't really surprise me when I found out She was a warrior Goddess (that was capable of taking any man to his knees), but I did find it interesting that she was associated with October 31st. My favorite holiday growing up was (and still is for that matter) Halloween and I believe I have been on the warrior path ever since I was a little kid. I've loved to wrestle and always considered myself strong and ready to fight when needed. I always played hard and reveled in my bruises and cuts as if they were trophies of my physical accomplishments. I never let anyone, particularly men, tell me what I could and couldn't do. I wanted to work in law enforcement all of my life, and in high school I was very active in my Junior Reserve Officer Training Unit; I was one of the first female (Air) Rifle Team Commanders, eventually working my way up to Commanding Officer of the unit. I was the protector of my friends and I was the girl you didn't mess with.

Many years later, after I had already determined that I would not have a need for a magical name She disagreed. For three days straight back in 2002 there were blackbirds of all kinds that seemed to follow me. Not only that, but songs would come on the radio or I'd notice songs on my CDs with the word blackbird somewhere in them. There would be tv shows or movies that would make reference to blackbirds and the final slap in the face was falling asleep to one movie on HBO and waking up to the part in I Am Sam when Sarah McLachlan's version of "Blackbird" plays (I had heard the Beatles version on the radio the day before as another one of my encounters in that three days). I finally got the clue and Sarah McLachlan's version has basically become my theme song. I have been Blackbird ever since.

Another affirmation of Her calling had to do with my birth name. While I won't reveal it here, my first name is sometimes equated with Cailleach, which in Gaeilge is used as a term for "witch" or "hag," and, in American books, my first name is associated with warriors. My family's surname is also connected with Co Kerry in Munster which, according to Celtic Heritage: Ancient Tradition in Ireland and Wales by Alwyn Rees and Brinley Rees, is the land of the dead/Otherworld. As if to bring this home, Cailleach Bheara is associated with Munster, but particularly Co Kerry, and there are times when her stories and the Morrigan's tend to overlap. The Cailleach's grandchildren are said to form the tribes associated with Kerry.

The Morrigan has continually reiterated her presence in my life. Not only was I married on Samhain in 2004, but I have dedicated myself to Her service and ritually re-dedicate myself to Her every Samhain.

Acquiescence
by Kim Cairelle Perilloux

The Dark Mare will not be denied;
Insistent gallop through my dreams.
The murder, flown in hallowed dust,
Alight on high with plots and schemes.

From lofty perch in canopy,
Cascade their cryptic words
Unbidden to my restless ear.
What say you, kindred birds?

I listen, rapt, to hear naught save
Veiled augury of passion.
Perchance, to mutter arcane prose
Akin to mine own fashion?

Yet still, o ruffled fiends, you mock,
Allude to destiny unknown.
Pray not forget your coal black sister
Bears stout burden of her own!

In frenzied past, I plucked the down,
Cast out the proffered feather.
Enlightened thus, now gather, sew
Plumed cloak to brook all weather.

As trembling needle binds the parts,
Beloved jesters, testify!
Your proclamations I do seek.
Reveal! Divinity draws nigh?

Assured or not, with onyx fringe
And hopeful sigh I fall to knee
At altar set with baited breath
Beneath the Black Queen's teeming tree.

The Morrigan
by Adrian Barlow

Cross the river of the otherworld
Enter her cave
See the cauldron bubbling away
See this mysterious woman dressed in red.

The Phantom Queen, the victorious warrior, the weaver of spells.
In magick she comes and goes;
Spying, watching all the time,
The undying force which reminds us all she is never far away.

In triple form we know her name,
But singular she can appear.
The oracle, caller of our destiny,
Collecting the fallen to fly again.

Samhain comes, the wheel turns, and the Veil thins.
The clock in the far off distance chimes midnight.
The Morrigan flies through the land,
Singing softly to her children;
Who are singing back in her praise.

Her sons and daughters gather at the fire
On top a hill on a moonlight Samhain night,
Wearing black feathers in their hair and dancing till the rising sun.
They spy three ravens sitting on a tree branch
And they know

THE MORRIGAN IS THERE!!!!!!!

Morrigan's Ride
by Gebirgsjägerinne

I will ride over the hills
made of fresh grass, covered with dew.
Red hair floating in the wind
like a fiery sword.

I will ride, and from my throat
the thunder howl will call the storm.
Let my cloak to float
over the morning mist.

I will ride without fear, naked and without shame.
I will ride relentlessly.
And my eyes will decide
who will live or die.

Raven's Wings
by Ophelia Anu

Treading a narrow trail through the unveiled trees
Night's veil has fallen, hiding their wailing bleakness
Feet shorn of shoes, with deadfall crackling underneath
Arms trembling in terror and legs buckling in weakness

Summoned by moonlight glaring a pale gaze in my room
I followed the ashen radiance outdoors without thought
Strangely unfettered by the strong fear that had bloomed
Comforted only when I moved toward what I knew not.

Now I find myself hiking through this spare wooded grove
Pulled by an intent, silent compulsion from within my mind.
Starlight, laced with dread, tightening the thin thread it wove
From my skin, onto the ground, and into the trees to unwind.

Lately have I paused on moments in life that I had rather forget
Languished quietly in luxurious apathy, ignoring the need
To progress, unfaltering, travel away from indulgent regret
Instead I gratified the pull of darkness and have let it breed.

Fired by an imagination full of bitterness and impotent rage
Sleeping the unawakened nightmare day by grudging day
Keeping the monstrosity at bay in its inadequate cage
I mired myself, steeped like tea leaves gone to rot and decay.

Lost to all but practicing the necessities, I have folded
Into a strangely comfortable sense of hollow misery.
Watched life, days, weeks pass as they slowly unfolded
And came to anticipate the numbness cloaking me eagerly.

Only this night I awoke again to the sour taste of bile
Filling my throat with all the words I wished I had spoken
Contorting, I lie in my womb of fetal malice a while
Before I am borne out into the night, stumbling and broken.

Muffled wing-beats fan the air and in a moment I know
That everything I thought true is about to permanently shatter
Darkness within darkness uncoils itself from deepest shadow
Eyes strain to see, night and sky receding, reality ceasing to matter.

Have I waited for her since I could think, watch their dark eyes
See my every step as life cradled me in its cold, alien embrace
Washed in the agony and the blood of the birthplace of lies
Set every principle on its side, every dark thought in its proper place.

Sat down hard from plain fear as if shoved onto the ground
I feel every twig and every stone that sits beneath my skirt
I listen, strain to hear any further evidence of her sound
As I struggle not to reach behind me to rub where I hurt.

A voice soft like falling leaves and sharp as flint shards
Cuts through the space between she and I; I am arrested
And the juxtaposition between the gentle and hard
Finds my tolerance and ability to think under duress sorely tested.

"Continue to deny a truth that has found you, have no doubt
it will harm you more than freeing this boiling gall
Confined venom will poison you from the inside out
And deplete your soul until there is nothing left at all."

Feeling small fissures begin to wend themselves around
The ghastly, bloodless walls of the crypt that I have built
A graveyard overwhelmed now begins to seep from the ground
Uncovering red thoughts that bury truth's sword in to the hilt.

Standing, I move forward to embrace the Truth and the Source
And with open arms She flies away, her arms turning black
Feathers catching the draft, setting her further course
And I follow after, never looking back.

Musings on the Irish War Goddesses
by Saigh Kym Lambert

Writing about the Morrígna and other related Irish War Goddesses is not an easy task for me. I've been largely reticent on the subject since I dedicated over two decades now, but during the past couple of years I have been compelled to begin writing on a combination of my research and experience with Them. There are a great many articles on the internet about *an Morrígan* already, from various NeoPagan sites, travel sites, and some academic material.

Many of the former two repeat some common misinformation that has developed. In the case of those who worship, some of this may or may not be valid Unsubstantiated Personal Gnosis (UPG),(1) but is often presented as if it were traditional material. Even when academic sources are used, they are typically from authors who are writing broadly and have not focused strongly on the extensive and confusing primary material about these Goddesses specifically.

There is also the matter of coding, the concept that any given audience to a story will interpret it according to its social and personal experiences, regardless of the messaging that the authors might have intended. This can change the story over time, as each writer offers his or her own interpretations as the actual story, sometimes leaving the actual intent far behind. This coding is something I feel should always be acknowledged, both to understand our own interpretations and those of others.(2) With the Irish material we not only have to consider our own social and personal codes and the likely ones of the original audience and writers, but also that of those scholars whose works we might also use.(3)

In light of this coding, I wish the reader to understand that I am coming from a particular viewpoint of a physical feminist and practicing Pagan on a warrior path, which includes magical and ecstatic practice as well as Reconstructionist methodology of informing experience with research. I have spent twenty-five years dedicated to a Goddess I know primarily as *an Morrígan*. Along with how I might read this material, I must keep in mind that this material was written not by Pagan warriors but by Christian clerics. I do not believe in a wide-ranging agenda to defame the Pagans, although some might have wished to,(4) but accept that these were not meant to preserve any pre-Christian concepts.

Importantly, I believe that these Goddesses are real, but acknowledge that some of the writers might not have any belief in Them at all. Others may have seen Them as "demonic," which I realize would be true to their own worldview. I do not believe in human written secret codes, but I do hold that perhaps the Gods Themselves use the texts to inform us. It's up to us to try to figure out what we can get through these stories, which are from the culture even as it was influenced by other cultures.(5) I believe we need to understand the culture that these tales came from, through various studies, and what we can of that which came before. There is a great deal of speculation in this, as well as UPG and Shared Personal Gnosis (SPG). I hope to try to stay clear when I am going in these directions. I will also work to show support for some of the theories I present and reasons why I make certain speculative leaps.

There is much that does not fit in the scope of this paper, details that would run too long. This is an attempt to write concisely, something some will feel this introduction already makes a failure. There is so much material and so much confusion that writing something brief about this group of Goddesses is nearly impossible, although a good attempt to do so has been done by Maya St. Clair in *"An Morrígan:* War Goddess and More."(6) What follows here is a truncation of a much larger project which I have been working on, and therefore there are many areas in which I could have gone into far more detail – and will, one day.

I: Defining the Queen

The name, or rather title, *"an Morrígan"* is probably a good place to start. There are many interpretations given. Whitley Stoke noted that the variation without the accent on the "o" in "Morrigan," which means "Phantom or Specter Queen," was more plentiful in the texts, and was also favored by many other scholars.(7) This would connect to related Indo-European words such as the Germanic and Nordic "mare" or "mara" ("specter") from which we get "nightmare," and which should not be mistaken for "mare" as in "female horse."(8) Stoke noted that the accent over the "o" that would lead to the translation of "Great Queen" was a later folk etymology, which is arguably where we mostly find it.(9) Máire Herbert favors "Mórrígan," which would appear to mean "Great Queen," claiming it more prevalent. But this seems based on a survey of place names, which would put it in folk etymology as Stokes has noted, as opposed to the literature.(10) Epstein also notes Kim McCone's assertion that the etymology actually relates to the Indo-European root for mer as in "one who is dead" or "slain," making Her Queen of the Slain.(11)

    I am highly persuaded by Stokes' assessment of what the earliest spellings define, and therefore this is the spelling I use here when not quoting something with a different spelling. It has been my observation that many who tend to prefer the spelling "Mórrígan" ("Great Queen"), usually those who wish to downplay Her warrior aspects, seem to interpret "mór" as "illustrious" rather than "big" as in the opposite of "bec" (or modern "beag") for "little." The word, like the English word "great," has both meanings.(12) Certainly, "the Big Queen" does seem fitting when looking at the fact that this spelling seems mostly connected to place-names, and that those items or body parts laid out in the landscape attributed to Her would certainly demonstrate that She was, indeed, of great size. While the spelling may not be prevalent in the literature, there are references that She could be physically large. One of the best known examples would be when She meets with the Dagda with a foot on each side of the River Unshin at the "The Bed of the Couple" ("Lige ina Lánomhnou' a ainm an baile ó sin").(13) I find that most folk etymology is about practical observation, even if having nothing to do with the original meaning of a word. One of the problems with the idea of it as the original meaning is that "mór" as an adjective is used after the name or noun it is describing, such as with Dagda Mór.(14)

Of course, this is only one name or title, and to Whom it applies is often a confusion in itself. Again, sorting it out completely may be beyond the scope of this article, possibly even impossible to accomplish completely. It should be noted that "morrígna," the plural, might be used not only for the Goddesses we're discussing but also for other women, usually supernatural in nature. Likewise, "badba" may also be used; it may mean "scald crow," "battle demon," or "witch," and at times seems to refer to possibly human witches, although such boundaries can be hard to establish.(15)

II: As Easy As 1, 2, 3?

Many see the Morrígan, or possibly the plural "Morrígna," as a generic name for a Triple Goddess, Who is Badb, Macha and Ananm; or Badb, Macha and the Morrigan; or Badb, Macha and Nemain; or Badb, Nemain and Bé Néit, depending on the source.(16) This becomes complicated at those times when They are more than three, as we'll see in a moment. Alternatively, Hennessey preferred "Badb" as being the overall title of the trio rather than "Morrígan."(17)The actual use of the definition of *an Morrígna* as a triple Goddess appears to have begun in the glosses, such as *O'Mulconry's Glossary* which are later than most of the tales.(18)

Due to the focus on triads, some NeoPagans continue to try to force the War Goddess(es) into Robert Graves' modern Maiden/Mother/Crone archetype, although more are beginning to realize the lack of historical evidence.(19) While the Morrígan, at least in *Táin Bó Cúailnge Recession 1*, appears as a young adult of reproductive age and as an old hag, there are no real "maiden" incarnations to be found.(20) This dual-age appearance, possibly linked to how Sovereignty appears, does have some tradition, however. We see Sovereignty appear to Niall of the Nine Hostages this way. Macha MonRuadh also tricks would-be kings in similar guise although the "aged" role is replaced with a young leper.(21)

Many scholars and Celtic Reconstructionists tend to counter the Maiden/Mother/Crone categorization by claiming that She is a triple Goddess of function, referencing Georges Dumézil's theory that all Indo-European cultures and their Deities were structured into sacral/sovereign, warrior and fertility/production functions. Again, this becomes awkward when they try to figure out which of the Three represents which particular function specifically, just as it was problematic for Dumézil himself when he tried to show that three different literary Machas each represented one of his functions.(22) John Carey argued that Dumézil's functions merged in each of these Machas: the Warrior acted as sovereignty, the Seer foresaw war and the Producer used magic to determine the effects of war.(23) Still, we see that the Morrígan also can be seen to combine all three functions in Her activities, spouting poetic prophecy, inciting warriors and offering victory, and concerning Herself with cattle and the land, as we'll explore below. Such neat categories are impossible to assign.

But Who bears the name in the literature? "*An Morrígan*" is used to represent one, or another, of three sisters, the second set of three daughters of the Goddess Ernmas, the first being Banba, Fotla and Ériu, in several entries of *Lebor Gabála Érenn*.(24) The listings vary, but Badb, Macha and the Morrígan – with the last being also named Anann(25) – appear several times and early, so these are the three names that I favor, as did MacAlister. Heijda argues strongly for it and Epstein seems to lean towards this as well.(26)

Anann, however, is seldom mentioned in general Irish myth commentary such as MacCana or Green, as we have seen. However, other variations include "Badb, Macha and Anann" (without the title "the Morrígan" referred to at all); "Badb, Macha, who is also the Morrígan, and Anann" and, oddly, variations of "the other three daughters, Badb and Macha and the Morrígan and Anann being the seventh."(27) Regarding the listings which give us this last foursome, MacAlister notes it is probably a transcription error,(28) and Heijda further explains how "i." (id est, "to wit") was likely mistaken and replaced with "7" (ocus, "and") by later transcribers(29) and it was likely originally "Badb and Macha and the Morrígan, who is Anann" as in earlier accounts, with the confused scribe possibly throwing in the "seventh daughter" to try to work out how to explain the "fourth of the three."

Of this set of the daughters of Ernmas, Badb is not listed as being *an Morrigan* in any of the entries in the *Lebor Gabála Érenn*. Instead it is in stories where the names or titles "Badb" and "Morrígan" are found linked and actually seem to be used interchangeably in the literature, as in the *Cath Maige Tuired*(30) and the *Tochmarc Emire* ("The Wooing of Emer").(31) In later glosses, we also see Macha noted as being defined both as "badb" and as one of the "tres mórrígna."(32) This means that, indeed, all three Goddesses – Badb, Macha and Anann – might well bear the title "*an Morrigan*." Or for that matter, They might also bear the title "an Badb." I admit that my preference for seeing *an Morrígan* as a more embracing title may well come from my own initial understanding.

It seems rather clear in the literature and genealogies, despite the switching of names and titles, that these are three distinct Goddesses who are sisters, not a single unit of three aspects. Yet, as noted just above, the later glosses refer to the Three Morrígna, which does indicate that the "Triple Goddess" concept is not completely modern, while still entering the material late. Heijda, for one, notes that she feels that these are separate beings, although at the same time the names were used interchangeably in the literature.(33)

My own impression is that there is not one Triple Goddess with three aspects, but Three Goddesses, sometimes more, as we'll see, Who are similar and Whose designations are transferable. The actual Beings are not interchangeable, however. It is we, being flawed humans, who often have trouble sorting it all out.

There are two other names often associated with *an Morrígan*: "Fea" and "Nemain." The latter is often, in fact, added to the Sisterhood(34) in some way by modern Celticists and many Pagans, and I admit that I had done this myself until reexamining the material, likely due to the number of influential scholars who do.(35) This may have begun with Hennessey, who gave "Badb" as the overall name of the three sisters and included Nemain with Macha and the Morrígan.(36) Usually, except when added as a fourth of a trio as Green manages to do,(37) the name replaces one of the others; usually Anann, who is seldom included in modern commentary. Sometimes Macha is left out as well and only the title the Morrígan is listed with Badb and Nemain.(38) However, Nemain and Fea are never listed as Daughters of Ernmas in the genealogies. Instead, in some listings They are said to be the Daughters of Elcmar, which in one of the listings is Ernmas' son, which would make Them nieces of Badb, Macha and the Morrígan/Anann.(39)

Even when this connection is not made, They are simply listed near, but not among, the Sisterhood, often as the Bé Néit (Wives of Néit). This is where the confusion probably stems, for Néit's wives are not always listed by the same names; They are usually a pair, although sometimes one but never three, and might be Fea and Nemain, Nemain and Badb, the Morrígan, Badb, or Nemain singularly.(40) Clark notes that the *Táin Bó Cúailnge Recession 1* mentions Nemain, Badb and Bé Néit shrieking over the troops and contends that this identifies the Morrígan as the triple Goddess made up of these three.(41) However, as Heijda discusses in some detail, it is likely that Badb and Nemain are the Bé Néit noted here.(42) However, Epstein and Heijda do not favor interpreting Nemain as a Sister in their studies, to which I am inclined to agree, while Heijda does feel that Fea is another name for Badb and likewise notes that Badb may well be seen as the overlapping member of two different collections of War Goddesses.(43)

The question of the Bé Néit being different Goddesses, as well as the number of similar Goddesses we are dealing with, could indicate the idea that we may be dealing with a clerical attempt to unify similar Territorial Goddesses into one family. It may be that Fea and Nemain, too, held the titles of either an Badb or *an Morrígan* or both among Their people. Even if They didn't hold these titles, They may have served such functions of Territorial War Goddesses. This, of course, is all theoretical; as I noted, we do not really know what the pre-Christian or early holdout Pagans believed, for it is not from them that we receive these tales.

III: Are They Even Goddesses?

There seem to be no references to any of this family as being Gods Themselves in the genealogies of the *Lebor Gabála Érenn*, aside from the Three Gods ("trí déo Danonn" Brian,

Iucharba, and Iuchair) who are mentioned as Annan's sons in one version.(44) Nor in the Mythological Cycle is such a title given specifically to the Sisters. However, there are references to *an Morrígan* as a Goddess in two other locations.

One is in the *Tochmarc Emire* passage which was referred to previously: "In the Wood of Badb, i.e. of the Morrigu, for that is her wood, viz. the land of Ross, and she is the Battle-Crow and is called the Wife of Néit, i.e. the Goddess of Battle, for Néit is the same as God of Battle."(45) It is noteworthy that She is specifically called a "Goddess of Battle" ("bandee in catæ") in this text, putting to rest the accusation that "War Goddess" was a pure invention of Hennessey.(46)

The other is in the *Metrical Dindshenchas*: "As busy dark-wrinkled Odras was sleeping in the early morning the Dagda's wife found her: in this wise came the shape-shifting goddess".(47) Within another tale from one of the Dindshenchas, Tulchaine prays to Her, asking that She steal his love's cattle, a rare example of anyone praying to Her or any of the other Tuatha Dé Danann.(48) Both these tales will be further discussed in the next section.

As I note above, a more difficult question to answer is whether any of these Goddesses, or most of the Tuatha Dé Danann for that matter, truly were pre-Christian Deities, as our sources are Christian. We get a cross-cultural hint of such a Goddess as Badb, however, in the Gaulish inscription "athuboduæ Aug[ustæ] Servilia Terenta [votum] s[olvit] l[ibens] m[erito]." Pictet interpreted the first word, with its first letter missing, as cathuboduæ and related it to the Irish Badb Catha.(49) While care must be given even when comparing different Celtic cultures, I think this similarity in light of the later Irish literature is indicative of the possibility.

As I noted in the beginning, this is Christian literature and not truly Pagan mythology. Therefore we do not and cannot know precisely what Pagan Gaels, either before or after Christianity became the dominant religion, believed about *an*

Morrígan or any of these related Goddesses or what they practiced due to this belief, as no practicing Pagan wrote it down. Yet it seems unlikely that these clerics invented Them out of whole cloth. (50) Instead, I believe that we do see hints of what Goddesses existed; possibly local territorial Goddesses, which the clerics may simply have been trying to understand within the context of their own world, which included many native and non-native concepts.

IV: Cows, Sovereignty and The Land

Many commentators, both scholars and NeoPagans, see a contradiction in a Goddess Who is connected to fertility, sovereignty and motherhood in any way, being a War Goddess as well. Some have worked hard to try to make a case that these Goddesses were originally peaceful, loving Earth Mothers until "the patriarchy" set out on a smear campaign against Them. For some scholars and most NeoPagans, this was done by the Christian clerics, while others claim that it was "Pagan hordes" who did this when they supposedly overran the peaceful monotheistic Goddess-culture that she seems to think existed beforehand.(51)

Of course, this is likely just an extreme reaction to the confusion that many other scholars have expressed about these Goddesses' apparent contradictory traits. Marie-Louise Sjoestedt was among those who found the idea of a sovereignty and fertility Goddess also being a War Goddess confusing.(52) John Carey described these Goddesses, focusing on Macha, as being dual: destruction and fertility. (53) Like the Dumézilian triad of function and the MMC concept, Carey's theory is an attempt to categorize the Goddesses in ways that I believe makes this too much of a conflict, rather than part of a natural cycle. The idea that Goddesses or Gods should not be as complex as people can be, with many attributes and connections, many interests and abilities, seems to be prevalent. But I feel that these apparent inconsistencies only serve to show the complex Beings with which we are dealing. This confusion may well relate to the common gender coding of these traits, something both the early Irish and many of the scholars likely believed.(54) But we also need to consider how the cycle of life works: life and death are one. We might also want to consider where warfare and fertility obviously connected for the Irish, within customs with their cattle.

It's easy, even for those who have no direct contact with the animal in question, to make a connection between cattle and fertility. Many make this cattle/fertility connection with the Morrígan's obvious interest in them.(55) Yet the connection of warfare and cattle, as seen in the *Táin Bó Cúailnge* and other cattle raid stories and also evident in other texts as well as archaeology, is also clear in the early Christian Irish culture, as it may have been in pre-Christian times.(56) This raiding would have actually played a fertility role, allowing opportunities for out-breeding different herds, some of which the raiders might consider better than their own. Sovereignty also connects into this, when we consider the *crech ríg*, ("king's raid") when a newly elected king would lead cattle raids into neighboring territories to both celebrate his office and prove his reputation.(57) In this way, cattle show this link between fertility and warfare; hence a Goddess connected to cattle would naturally be connected to both functions.

This link is seen in two related foretales (remscéla) to the *Táin Bó Cúailnge* which have *an Morrígan* involved with cows. Breeding plays a part in that a calf is involved, but so is war, as She steals a cow in order to start the *Táin Bó Cúailnge* and make Her favored warrior's fame. In the *Táin Bó Regamna*, the Morrígan steals a cow to breed to the Donn Cúailnge ("Brown Bull of Cooley," the bull Medb makes the raid for in TBC). Cú Chulainn tries to stop Her, but She mocks and insults him by telling him that he will die in a cattle raid when the calf the cow carries is a year old. This gets him worked up, boasting that he will be remembered forever for this raid and that he will survive the event. As it's unlikely She would make a false prophecy, this would seem to be Her intent, to get him to want to make his name through this raid.(58)

In *Echtrae Nerai*, the Morrígan's stealing of this cow and Cú Chulainn's interference is noted more concisely, for this is the story of the resulting calf's boasting about his father which helps entice Medb to take on the raid to see if the Donn could indeed best her husband Aillel's Finbennach (Whitehorn).(59) The Morrígan plays no actual role in this, only Her previous involvement with breeding of the calf is noted. So we see fertility, but even that breeding seems to be primarily to get the *Táin* started.

The two other tales involving *an Morrígan* and cows are the two from the Dindshenchas noted in the last section relating to Her identity as a Goddess. They are not connected specifically to warfare, but do involve stealing cattle; only the first relates to cattle breeding, however. In the tales naming the river Odras, a bull She is herding steals some of the cows under the care of a woman named Odras.(60) This brave, but quite foolhardy young woman confronts the "…shape-shifting goddess" to retrieve her cows. In the *Metrical Dindshenchas* version, she even tries to challenge Her in armed combat.(61) *An Morrígan* turns her into the river while she sleeps.

In the other tale, it is the one example of prayers being offered to Her. A druid, Tulchaine, asks Her to steal the cattle of his Otherworldly beloved, Dil, in order that the Sídhe woman would leave her mound to be with him.(62) While neither of these stories lead to war, Her main involvement is with stealing, an activity which seems to interest Her greatly. This is also the only time She seems to get involved with another's sex life rather than Her own, which indicates the supposed "Sex Goddess" label applied by many NeoPagans does not fit, as that would imply regular interfering with others.

Her own sexuality is obvious, and has a link to Sovereignty, as seen in Her meeting with the Dagda.(63) Interestingly, it is victory She offered rather than kingship. Her interest in Cú Chulainn, when She attempts to seduce him as the daughter of Búan in *Táin Bó Cúailnge Recession 1*, is likely an offer of similar victory. He refuses this offer and chooses to create his own glory rather than take an easy win.(64) What many claim is an act of rage, when She comes against him as a wolf, heifer and eel, can also be read as bringing him greater fame by bringing greater odds against him. Yet this hardly conflicts with the role of Sovereignty in general, as proper kingship was supposed to bring victory in any given war. She just seems to be more active about it than Sovereignty is usually accepted as doing.

We also see one of the Machas take on the role of Sovereignty, when Macha Mongruadh entices the sons of one of her defeated enemies into the woods by posing as a leper, in an allusion to the tale of Niall of the Nine Hostages.(65) These would-be kings, however, were captured by Macha one by one. Again, the role of Sovereignty, typically viewed as the ultimate "inactive" position for a Goddess, is turned into something not only active, but very aggressive. These tales lend an interesting twist to the concept and question the assumption of passive sovereignty. It also is interesting that this Macha was obviously meant to be a human, perhaps giving a hint of a queen standing in for a Goddess and literally taking on the role of Sovereignty which, in this instance, she keeps for herself rather than giving to a king.

As Sovereignty, we also see a connection with the land, something that Herbert emphasizes.(66) Certainly we see many landmarks attributed to Her, as noted above. As Sovereignty, it is true that She is likely a territorial Land Goddess. Many NeoPagans may well mistake this concept for an Earth Mother Goddess archetype that is not the same thing and may not be found in Celtic culture at all. Territorial Goddesses mating with the Tribal God are supposed to unite one particular people with one area of land,(67) rather than being the all-encompassing Earth. This may be a reason why these Goddesses are so confused and confusing. Could the scribes have been trying to make unity by making similar Goddesses from various locations into a single family?

When considering the Earth Goddess concept and all the place-names, it should also be remembered that naming was a great concern to the Gaels. There are a multitude of place-name (Dindshenchas) manuscripts, which include places named for both male and female figures. In most of these places there are several possible stories offered involving various figures, which may not all be the same gender. In relationship to many of the Morrígan or Mórrígan locations, there are ones attributed to An Dagda and other members of His family, both male and female.(68) Likewise, claims(69) that She is a domestic Hearth Goddess due to the late name of the *Fulacht na Morrígna*, a large Burnt Mound, must also be considered in light of the fact that smaller Burnt Mounds are often called *Fulacht Fian* "Cooking Place of the Fiana" or *Fulacht Fiadh* "Wild (or deer) Hearth" connecting them to the Fianna, which never seem to be therefore called "Outlaw Bands of Chefs" for it. These apparent "cooking spots" were seen as "wild" and linked in the folk mind to warbands, rather than being seen as domestic kitchens.(70) And the largest, of course, must belong to the "Big Queen" Who also may be seen as of the wild.

V: Mommy Greatest?

It is perhaps "Mother" that is the most difficult part for many to resolve with the warrior side. It seems many cannot conceive that a Goddess or woman could be both. This surprises some mothers I know, some who have themselves gone to war. Yet, despite the fact that human women can be both mother and soldier, you see many who claim that the Morrígan is a Mother Goddess and therefore cannot be a War Goddess.

Oddly, few making these claims ever seem to note that She is Annan, or of the connection typically made of Annan with the *Danu, considered by many to be the mother of all the Tuatha Dé Danann. In fact, it is in one of the listings from *Lebor Gabála Érenn IV* where the Morrígan is identified with the Paps of Annan that She is linked also to Danann, or *Danu. Here She is listed in the genealogy as the mother of three of Her father's sons, who are known as "tri dee dána" often translated as "the Three Gods of *Danu,"(71) but which Carey notes may actually mean "the Three Gods of skill."(72)

However, in this case the entry also claims that her name "Danann" is given to the Tuatha Dé Danann, although it does not indicate if She is Mother to all the Tuatha Dé ("The Morrigu, daughter of Delbaeth, was mother of the other sons of Delbaeth, Brian, Iucharba, and Iuchair: and it is from her additional name "Danann" the Paps of Ana in Luachair are called, as well as the Tuatha De Danann.").(73) Another listing, one of the ones which lists Anann as the fourth daughter, then refers to her as "Danann" and as "mother of the Gods. ("Badb and Macha and Morrigu and Ana, of whom are the Paps of Ana in Luachair, the three daughters of Ernmas the she-husbandman. That Dana is mother of the gods, and these are her daughters, Airgden, Barrand, Be Chuille, Be Thete".)(74) Anann is also listed as being Danann in the 10th century *Cormac's Glossary* as "mother of the Gods."(75)

However, the *Cath Maige Tuired Cunga* ("The First Battle of Moytura")(76) and the *Cath Maige Tuired*(77) clearly show Danann as separate from the Morrígan, but as united with Her in the effort of the wars. To make this more fun, we have a version of the Banshenchas, which not only lists "Badb, the wife of the great Dagda. Anand, that is, the Morrígan, from whom the Two Breasts of Ana in Luachair Deadad are named, was the other wife of the Dagda"(78) separately from Danann, but gives new life, as it were, to the word "Dé," typically translated as "Deity," by stating that "De and Danand the two goddesses, from whom Túatha De and Danand was [named], (and they are not identical and their kings were the Great Dagda and Lug, etc.), were the two wives of Tuireand Bicreand."(79) It seems clear that there was no consensus on whether Anann and Danann were the same or different, which was the Mother of the Gods or, in this last example, how many Tuatha were involved. This makes it even less clear as to what we might believe regarding whether They are the same.

The other issue is with the entire concept of *Danu as the Primal Mother as we have come to see Her, which has been reasonably questioned by John Carey and Alexei Kondratiev.(80) When it comes to the idea of *an Morrígan* as the Primal Mother, it should be considered that the primary evidence that She is "Mother of the Gods" lists Her own mother before Her.(81) Either way, there is truly no evidence in the tales that either the Morrígan/Anann or Danann were a primal progenitor, nor is there any suggestion of any such Goddess. Even the naming of the Tuatha Dé Danann at its most literal suggests they are named for Her and mother of some, but not that She is the mother of all.

The *Sanas Cormaic* ("Cormac's Glossary") from the 10th century has a second reference to Anann as "mother of Gods" and Buanann as apparently both mother (máthair) and foster-mother (muimme) of heroes or warriors.(82) Moreover, this connection of Anann, the Morrígan, with the name or title "buanann" is particularly interesting, as we'll discuss later on in regards to the foster-mothers of Cú Chulainn and Finn Mac Cumhail. This notes the connection of Anann with the name Buanann, who is the mother or foster-mother of warriors specifically.

"Buanann nurse* of the heroes, i.e. be n-Anann (a) from their similarity to each other, for as the Ánu was mother of gods, sic Buanann erat mother of the heroes i.e. a good mother.

Aliter Buan-ann [,i. daghmatair c good mother' B.] the buan i.e. is bón i.e. from bonum, as is said genither
buan ó ambuan e buan is born from ambuan' i e. good from evil. The ann that is in Buanann denotes mater. It is this that is in Ana [Anand B] i.e. mater deorum. Buanann then (means) a good mother for teaching feats of arms to the heroes."(83)

We do know that *an Morrígan* was mother of Meche, who had three serpents in his heart. If He had lived, they would have grown to such a size as to destroy Ireland, so He was killed by Mac Cecht to prevent this.(84) Interestingly, other than the mere fact that She was His mother, *an Morrígan* is not mentioned. She never comes forward with either motherly vengeance or grief in this story. The relationship apparently is noted only to identify Meche.

When looking at the other Sisters, we again see a Macha, this time ingen Sainrith meic Inboith, who Dumézil considered the Mother aspect. Yet motherhood only comes at the end of the story, in some versions just before She dies, never mothering those children.(85) Therefore childbirth is also where She curses the Ulstermen to suffer the pangs of childbirth at times of danger to their territory, involving Herself completely with the events of the *Táin Bó Cúailnge* and other conflicts. As Epstein wrote, "Once again, even in the act of motherhood, one of the morrígna is enmeshed in armed conflict."(86) Again, we have to consider that while clearly Otherworldly, we can't be certain this Macha was truly ever to be considered a Goddess.

Another link to *an Morrígan* as mother is absolutely in regards to Her role as a War Goddess and, for me, a very inspirational, if seemingly minor, reference. In the Fenian tale *Acallamh na Senórach* ("The Colloquy of Old Men") among a list of the Tuatha Dé Danann who attack Donn mac Midir every year are "the children of the Morrígan daughter of Ernmais, with her twenty-six female warriors and her twenty-six male warriors."(87) As Epstein points out, the term used here, "clann," although it often has a familial meaning, was also used to indicate a warband. Therefore the translations of "children" may be more literal than the original meaning.(88) It's an intriguing passage for me, however, in that whether these are Her children or a warband dedicated to Her, half of them are female and it seems to be the largest force of female fighters to be found in the literature.

VI: Sorcery and Sight

Magic, specifically destructive, is typically part of the Morrígan's and Her Sisters' powers. It is, in fact, seen by many to be the "femininely" acceptable form of warfare that They practice, leading many to deny that They ever fight physically, as if one negates the other. Yet the Tuatha Dé Danann, male and female, are largely defined as magic users and the use of magic never seems to negate that any of the male Gods fought physically. Noteworthy is the Dagda, who is a "god of wizardry"(89) as well as a warrior. He promises Lugh that He will fight both physically and magically in the Second Battle,(90) and certainly displays both talents in both *Cath Maige Tuired* tales among others. The physical exploits of the Goddesses might be downplayed by the original transcribers, but it is not surprising for as Bitel noted in a more general context, legal documents reflect a belief that physical violence by women, except towards children and other women, was not an concern. However, harm by a woman using sorcery was of much greater concern.(91)

In the *Cath Maige Tuired Cunga Badb*, Macha and the Morrígan do send forth clouds of mist and rains of fire and blood upon the Fir Bolg to keep them from resting for days before the physical battle at which They, Their three elder sisters and their two foster-mothers, Danann and Be Chuille, are among the list of warriors.(92) It's not explicitly noted that these Goddesses fight, but as They are listed among the male warriors who are assumed to fight, it seems a stretch to claim They didn't. In the Second Battle, Bechuille and Danann are the ones offering magical aid, as do Druids and the Dagda, the last offering both. The Morrígan's offer is more vague in regards to method; what isn't vague is Her bloodthirstiness in Her promise, and like Dagda, may well mean both.(93) She does offer magical incitement and prophecy, yet doing so alone does not negate any other activity.(94)

Along with sorcery, another of the Morrígan's powers includes prophecy, including foreseeing the dire end of the world after the *Cath Maige Tuired*.(95) Earlier in the tale, She also tells the Dagda where the Fomoire will be landing, which She may know due to this gift.(96) In the *Táin Bó Cúailnge* She even appears to the Donn Cúailnge, Brown Bull of Cooley, to warn him of the raid.(97) While She is often proclaimed a Goddess of prophecy, it seems actual accounts are limited, even some of the times She supposedly uses these talents with Cú Chulainn. We must either conclude She can be wrong, or, as I believe more likely, She was actually working to incite him, such as in Her proclamation in *Táin Bó Regamna*, that he will die during the raid, although it could be interpreted that She instead intends Her hero to make his name.(98)

We see both magic and the Sight used by other warriors in the literature, including women warriors. The skill of imbas forosnai is also found in women-warriors, at least the teachers, such as Finn's foster, Bodbmall(99) including Cú Chulainn's teacher, Scáthach.(100) We get a brief glimpse also at the death of Símha inghen Chorrluirgnig, who is referred to as "…badhb & ban-ghaisgedach do muinntir Ghuill í…" "…witch (101) and warrior-woman in Goll's retinue…."(102) Yet it's not only female warriors, for the prime example of a warrior-seer is Finn himself.(103) This may well indicate the concept of a warrior who also uses magic, which we also see in Cú Chulainn's use of ogam(104) as well as his ríastrad, which I believe should be counted as battle-magic. So while it is clear that magic and prophecy are used by Goddesses and female warriors, we see they are also practiced by male warriors. Yet many seem to see the use of magic by female warriors as proof that they are wholly supernatural and never fight physically, while male warriors apparently can use both.(105)

VII: Physical Battle

Do They ever fight physically? Most scholars, as noted above, seem to fully believe They did not, something it seems that Epstein alone questions.(106) The truth is that while there is no explicit description of any of the Daughters of Ernmas fighting, this is true of many of the male Tuatha Dé Danann, with only a few of the battles being described. The exception to this is, of course, when *an Morrígan* fights Cú Chulainn physically, in the forms of wolf, eel and heifer,(107) which is clearly a physical battle. While the shape-shifting aspect might throw some who do not believe in such things, it should be remembered that not only is She "the shape-shifting" Goddess, but She may well be associated with "shape-shifting" warriors, including Cú Chulainn. Therefore the fact that She is in animal form should not be contrary to this having been a physical confrontation.

Other descriptions are more roundabout; the actual physical fighting is not described, but sometimes is quite clearly present. The clearest would be Macha Mongruadh taking the sons of Dithorba one by one using trickery, but it's as likely they were then subdued physically as in any other way.(108) This is problematic, as noted above, in that this Macha may not be the Goddess; however, Macha, Daughter of Ernmas, is listed as dying at the hand of Balor in the *Cath Maige Tuired*,(109) indicating She may have been as much a participant as the God Nuada is assumed to be. Badb and Nemain, as Bé Néit, likewise die with Néit at Ailech, which may well mean They were combatants as well. (110) In the *Cath Maige Tuired Cunga,* Badb, Macha and the Morrígan clearly do use magic to fight as noted above, but later on They and other Goddesses are listed along with male warriors as They go into Battle, leaving it open to interpretation. My own interpretation is that both male and female Deities used both magic and physical force, as we see so often in the mythology when it comes to men fighting.(111)

While the Goddesses definitely have other means of warfare, such as the magic and prophecy we mentioned before, as well as the shrieking over the battlefields of the *Táin Bó Cúailnge,*(112) there is no actual statement of whether They did or did not take part in actual fighting. That is aside from the battle with Cú Chulainn at the ford. There are hints, but the evidence may be too open to personal belief and there is no way to ever claim complete proof whether They did or did not.

VIII: Psychopomps and Death Messengers

One of the most common attributions given *an Morrígan,* Badb and Macha in NeoPaganism is that of "Death Goddesses." Epstein certainly notes Their possible psychopomp roles, relating them to the Valkyries,(113) and Matthias Egler explores the Irish War Goddesses along with similar "devourers" of those violently killed in other cultures.(114) The relationship between these Goddesses and carrion birds surely seen eating the dead on the battlefield makes the connection strong, as does the Badb/Crow who oversees Cú Chulainn's death. The Washer at the Ford, foretelling of the death of those who see Her washing their clothing, appears in the literature to warriors as well.(115) Like the Valkyrie, it seems that the dead that interest these Goddesses are the slain warriors, with no indication of an interest in guiding others to the next world.

The identity of the Washer at the Ford can be another confusing element to this exploration, however, especially as seen at Cú Chulainn's death.(116) Within this section we have *an Morrígan*, who appears to be trying to prevent his death, the Daughter(s) of Cailitín also called "Badb" getting him to break his geis and obviously wanting his death, and Badb's daughter "ingin Baidbi"(117) who is the Washer at the Ford. These many references to "Badb" can create a confusing picture of a single being trying to save him, trying to kill him, and mourning his death. Both Epstein and Heijda see Cailitín's daughters as clearly separate from being the Goddess,(118) but do connect the Washer with the Morrígan, according to Epstein, or the Badb, according to Heijda.(119) However, could this not be a third supernatural being, in fact the Goddess Badb's daughter, Who also has an interest in Her mother/aunt's charge? There is another reference to Badb's Daughter found in the *Táin Bó Cúailnge Book of Leinster*, where Fergus notes her land is where many men will be killed by Cú Chulainn.(120) Perhaps it is not Badb, but Her daughter who is Washer, adding to a complex interrelation of beings.

In later folkloric traditions, there are death messengers who proclaim non-violent deaths specifically, yet many connect them to the War Goddesses due to the Washer at the Ford.(121) However popular this link might be, it appears fairly tenuous, and it may well be that there were always various beings concerned with the deaths of certain people. What may have changed is not the nature of the messengers, as Lysaght implies, but rather which types of deaths, people and messengers became of interest in the stories. That the War Goddesses are concerned with death is obvious; that They might be the only ones who are concerned is a stretch considering the number of ways in which people might die in a warrior culture.

IX: A Goddess of Women

This is a new one for me, but I've seen it on so many websites that *an Morrígan* is a woman's Goddess, some adding that She is concerned especially with abused women and children. Therefore I determined that the concept needs exploring. It does seem that a lot of Her modern devotees are women, although I know a good number of men who serve Her as well. However, in terms of precedence from the texts, this isn't evident.

Certainly Badb, Macha and Annan seem to work together, perhaps with Fea and Nemain, and in the *Cath Maige Tuired Cunga* ("The First Battle of Moytura" or "Battle of Maige Tuired at Cong") with several other Goddesses.(122) This could indicate a good relationship between Them, in a body of literature where women, especially women of the same status, often are in conflict with one another.(123) It might be said They might offer some example of the strength of sisterhood many of us seek. The direct interaction with human women in the literature, what little we have, is not typically very positive, however.

We've already noted Her answering a man's prayers to bring his intended bride out of her Sídhe, which does not indicate how Dil felt about the entire situation other than not wanting to leave her bull. Yet, it hardly seems she was too happy about the whole thing or that it was in her best interest. Odras, obviously, did not fair well at the Morrígan's hands.

The only other interaction between one of these Goddesses, Badb, and a woman is not quite so confrontational and could be read to offer vengeance to a wronged woman, Medb. But at the same time Badb is seen inciting the man, Conchobar, to again grievously wrong her. This is in *Tochmarc Ferbe* ("The Wooing of Ferb"), another foretale of the *Táin Bó Cúailnge* and like the tales of the Brown Bull's calf, it shows a

War Goddess in the role of inciter of the upcoming battle.(124) In version II of the tale, the apparition who appears to both Conchobar and Medb is noted only as the "White Lady" or "Pale One" although there are references in other parts of this version to Badb, which links Her to these terms. In version I, She is actually identified as Badb when She appears to Medb. The rhetorical exchange used in Leahy's translation is actually from version II, but the naming of Badb in that meeting is added from version I.(125) Badb tells the sleeping Conchobar about the cattle raid, but also that Medb's son, Mani Morgor, has gone to be Ferb's holding with a retinue of one hundred and fifty. Conchobar's "glorious deed" is to gather three hundred warriors and attack them. She then visits Medb in her sleep to tell her that her son will be killed by Conchobar's attack and prompts her towards vengeance.(126)

There is little here, in this only apparent exchange between one of the War Goddesses and a woman, to indicate any special relationship or concern for Medb's suffering. Badb clearly is inciting both Medb and Conchobar further into their hostilities, at the expense of Medb's son. There is no indication of Badb actually helping Medb against the wrongs Conchobar has done. It comes back to starting a war which appears to exist exclusively to glorify Cú Chulainn.

Of course, the literature was not written by or for women, so what relationships women might have had with these Goddesses we cannot truly know. Of course, we have few real tales telling of interactions with a Deity and Cú Chulainn's experiences with *an Morrígan* are a rare example in the literature of what might be interpreted as a relationship with a patron Deity. Sadly, there are no such superlative female examples, although we may be able to extrapolate evidence, especially in relationship to a warrior woman who is Cú Chulainn's teacher.

We have already seen that there are five Machas and not all seem to be Goddesses. One, Macha Monruadh, appears to be a human queen and a warrior, who also enacts the role of Sovereignty. Could it not be that a queen, should there be a titular one (of which she and Medb seem to be alone, and considered completely fictional)(127) would actually stand in for the Sovereignty Goddess, perhaps even taking Her name (or be given it later on)? If we believe this is the case, it would indicate a relationship between these queens and the Goddesses in question.

While some read Scáthach as likely having been a Goddess turned human(128) or at least Otherworldly,(129) I feel there is more reason to read her as a human prophetess and possibly priestess.(130) That she bears the title Buanann at one point in the *Táin Bó Cúailnge Book of Leinster*(131) could either confirm her status as a former Goddess or that she might be priestess to such a Goddess; that a priestess would be a "reflection" of a Goddess is, of course, a provocative reading, especially given her name.(132) She shares both warrior arts and prophetic skills with *an Morrígan* or Badb, she is teacher to Her favorite, and neither have a completely comfortable relationship with him, all of which point to the idea that she is a reflection and therefore perhaps priestess of such a War Goddess. Similarly, Nagy and Epstein both link Finn's foster-mother and teacher Bodbmall, both a warrior and a seer who becomes adversarial toward Finn when he leaves, to the War Goddess Buanann as *"muimme nafiann."*(133) Epstein also suggests that there may well be an etymological relationship between Bodbmall and Badb.(134) Either of these readings, that this is the Goddess given another identity or that she is a priestess, could be seen here. Such a distinction might be hard to sort out completely.(135) Might also the choice, as noted previously, of the label "badb" for the female Fiann member Símha inghen Chorrluirgnig offer such a similar hint? This is an evocative connection, although impossible to make concrete, to consider of the idea of warrior-priestesses in the warbands, as we go to the next topic.

X: Patron Goddess

While the stories are from Christian sources, some of us who follow the Morrígan do see what could be interpreted as a relationship between a Patron Goddess and a follower in Her interactions with Cú Chulainn. As Epstein notes, cautiously, this does not mean that there was a Warrior Cult dedicated to Her or that Cú Chulainn was meant to be presented as Her devotee in such a cult, but it is suggestive that if there was such a cult, he probably was thought to be part of it and She probably was the deity involved.(136) We must, however, also take caution that Cú Chulainn was not an "average" warrior and cannot truly be representative of an "average" follower of any such Goddess, even beyond the fact that those writing the tales probably had little, if any, knowledge of how a Pagan warrior might have interacted with a Deity. He was unique and probably meant to be a caricature of a warrior. A tribal warrior who is utterly liminal and in all ways an outsider, youthful yet skilled, out of control yet accepted, he did not fit, inside or outside.(137) We are not Cú and we really shouldn't try to be, but we can take lessons in his tale.

Their relationship has often confused both scholars and NeoPagans, as it seems *an Morrígan* is at times concerned for Cú Chulainn and at other times seems to despise him; and most read his reaction to Her as simply petulant and rude. For those coming from a non-warrior background, this is likely very bewildering.(138) We find Her taunting him not only in the *Táin Bó Regamna* and after he refuses Her advances in *Táin Bó Cúailnge Recession 1*,(139) but in his *Boyhood Deeds* (*Macgnímrada*), which are included in the *TBC Rec 1*. Then Badb taunts the boy when he faces a phantom: "Poor stuff to make a warrior is he who is overthrown by phantoms!" (*"Olc damnae laích fil and fo chossaib aurddrag!"*) This sparks his fury inciting him to win.(140) As MacCana and Epstein have noted, Her verbal attacks are more along the lines of gressacht, incitement by ridicule, which is found throughout the Ulster tales.(141) We also see this performed at the warrior's insistence by Cú Chulainn's charioteer during the TBC.(142)

Likewise, by attacking him physically while he fights in the *Táin Bó Cúailnge,* She is offering him more glory, for an easy victory is wasted on such a champion.(143) Again, it has become fairly common to see NeoPagans who say that his mistake was to refuse Her advances, incurring Her wrath, even though only one version has the scenario of Her offering him sex.(144) It seems more likely that when She offered sex, especially as She included the offer to help him win, She is offering victory, an easy victory unbecoming of a hero. It is something that Dagda might have been willing to take to win *Cath Maige Tuired* for Their people, but for Her chosen hero it might have brought about true anger, disappointment that he'd chose the easy way. Her attacks themselves serve to show that he was the greater champion, overcoming his foe while hampered by Her; his healing of Her afterwards glorifying his other abilities.(145)

Another aspect of Cú Chulainn's connection with Her would be his *ríastrad* or "battle fury" which would overtake him, causing him to become so enraged that his body would warp and he'd be unable to distinguish friend from foe.(146) Epstein connects this with the *berserkr* ("bear coats") and *ulfheðnar* ("wolf coats") who served Odin in Northern European cultures, and that *an Morrígan* is responsible for his transformation.(147) Epstein theorizes that this fugue state, both Cú's and the berserkr's is caused by actual Deity possession, the Morrígan and Odin respectively. I do not find any suggestive evidence that this is the case in the material, and as we'll discuss shortly, I have my own reasons to not see it as a Deity possession. I do think it is correct that it is an altered state, a fugue, and likely part of a cultic religious transformation. It is simply the Deity possession with which I disagree.

This sort of fugue, always alluding to shape-shifting in the literature, certainly would seem to be a gift bestowed by "the shape-shifting goddess." I believe it also must be related to the *fáelad* (wolfing) of the Fíanna and díberga, the Outlaw Warrior bands we also see in Ireland.(148) Although any connection that these followers are of a cult to *an Morrígan* or another Goddess of such nature is conjecture, I do feel that the evidence bears out that this is a distinct possibility. She takes, among others, the form of a wolf. While Cú Chulainn's *ríastrad* may not seem wolfish, he is "Hound." One might also note that while the usual interpretation of his tri-colored hair(149) is from bleaching caused by the use of lime, this tri-coloration is also suggestively canine. As the latter relates to his general appearance rather than his appearance during the fugue, it may be considered that he is always houndish. The importance of such altered states in warfare seems obvious, whether one attributes an actual supernatural enhancement or merely the more mundane explanation of focus and repression of fear. Another theory is that the altered state was created through the use of psychotropic substances, which might create hallucination, a sense of invulnerability, and a lack of pain response.(150)

The concept of the díberga/Fianna bands as possible cults to these War Goddesses, in which perhaps many youths passed but only a few remained,(151) is for me further suggested by the female teachers and foster-mothers we've discussed already. With the shared names/titles and related skill sets, whether one chooses to see them as priestesses or humanized Goddesses, they may further demonstrate such a devotion to these or similar War Goddesses. We are again hampered by the fact that there are relatively brief references to these women, but they are evocative nonetheless. We may also see a suggestion of this in the clann na Morrigna in the *Acallamh na Senórach*, for while these warriors may be supernatural members of the Tuatha Dé Danann, they may hint at the concept of Her children as warrior bands which may have been reflected in this world.(152)

XI: Worshipping With the War Goddesses Today

This is where I'll get heavily into UPG and SPG, based on belief and experience. Not all will agree, but I hope that I can demonstrate where some of this fits interpretations of what we know. It is beyond the scope of this article to go into full detail of how I worship the War Goddesses; it is beyond the scope of my interest or ability to offer an all-encompassing approach for how anyone might worship Them. As I have noted, this is from a warrior path viewpoint. I know no other, and I do not know how one who is not on this path might approach *an Morrígan*. This is not to say they shouldn't; only that it's not something I know. We do see the druid, Tulchaine, praying to the Morrígan; but again, that only tells us about asking Her to steal our Otherwordly love interest's cattle and it may not apply to many devotees today.

Tulchaine also may represent someone who is not dedicated to *an Morrígan* in particular. I do not believe that everyone must dedicate to particular Deities now or in the past, any more than someone who does so dedicate needs to ignore Others. And as we see that most entered the Fianna during their youth before being reaccepted into society, and probably Christianity, dedication may not be lifelong.(153) Therefore, some may have need of Her even if they do not have a lifelong dedication to her. I do suggest, however, that you might not want to petition the Morrígan for help with your love life unless it can be aided by the theft of cows.

To me, dedicating to *an Morrígan* involved dedicating to walk the warrior path. This included taking up physical training, including combat arts I never would have considered previously. While I had long been interested in fitness, my training became far more focused on power, strength, speed, and size (as in gaining, not losing) than just health, which I believe one needs to develop as a base for all else, just the same. Likewise, an interest in wilderness survival took on a whole new meaning for me.

I began training in the martial arts, seeking the most realistic training as I could find. Over the years, this also turned my previous discomfort with guns into what might be considered a bit of a fanaticism. I have some defensive training with handguns and it is a priority to continue to grow these skills. I feel it should be obvious that the warrior path is a very physical one.

This doesn't mean that it is without magic and spirituality, or that some of us might not be both *"…badhb & ban-ghaisgedach…"* "…witch and warrior-woman…." In fact, I think there is very much a place to be warrior-witches, to use various means both magical and spiritual. There are hints of this in the lore, with Símha inghen Chorrluirgnig, with Bodhmall, with Scáthach's prophecies, as well as Cú Chulainn and Fionn, with the magic warfare of the Goddesses Themselves.

These practices cannot be used without grounding in physical training for both fitness and combat. In the altered states, you cannot fugue with a body too weak to handle it, nor can you fugue your way through a fight if your body is unfamiliar with fighting.

The actual practice of battle-magic, seership, and fugue states is too complex to go into fully and is difficult for me to write about. Certainly the first is far more aggressive, offensive and "negative" than most NeoPagans prefer. It can involve dealings with Otherworldly beings or other people and does include forms of cursing most Pagans like to deny exist, let alone admit to practicing. On the other hand, it may include protection spells, invocations for aid, and dedications to the

Goddesses. We know little of the actual formulas that might have been used. The stories tend to describe the outcomes and were written by those who may have thought such practices demonic. This makes developing our own training in these things often difficult from a cultural perspective, especially as there is some shying away from magic among many in the CR movement, with some on professional warrior paths having other reasons to avoid altered states.

Seership skills, especially through the use of scrying and the reading of omens, may be more natural talent than learning. But there are more hints in the material in which the skills might be acquired or strengthened. The practices of the tarb feis and imbas forosnai(154) are of growing interest to many in the CR community. The covering of the head in both of these practices is something some of us have practiced. However, modifications from the exact information we have on them are typically made. Both involve the idea of eating or chewing on meat, but the boiled beef of the tarb feis is more acceptable than the unsafe raw pig meat of the imbas forosnai, let alone the dog or cat meat no one sane would chew on today – although we probably are not going to sacrifice a bull each time. We might also take inspiration from Finn's tale and eat salmon prior to trance instead. The act of chewing on fingers or thumb might easily be replicated.(155)

Battle frenzy, whether fáelad or ríastrad, is also difficult to describe. It might be viewed differently by different people, and it's often difficult to translate these experiences into language.(156) The first issue is the concept, which is not helped by Cú Chulainn's entertaining issues with reining it in, and the fact that it is described as "frenzy" or "fury" implying that it is about uncontrolled anger and rampage and nothing more. This makes for good stories and much fear-mongering, and the danger of it exists and can't be denied. But it is also about the removal of outside influences and fear, coming into "now time" and the use of the weapon-body at its most focused. Someone out of control and angry may claim that they are in this fugue state, but really, without the focus and the mental and physical training behind it, they're just out of control. I will say from my own experience that it is not Deity possession; possession of something, perhaps, but not by *an Morrígan*. It might be best described as possession by something deeper within myself.

The fugue state does not change the shape of our bodies, but may offer strength or at least better use of strength. It may even change the "feel" to some extent. It does require a trained body, one that is so familiar with the movement that will be needed that thinking about it is not required, as thinking about it only slows the body down. As both magical battle and ecstatic states require a trained body, and as not all who serve *an Morrígan* will practice these ways, it again comes to the importance of training physically.

We certainly do not know the exact methods of ancient Gaelic fitness training, but we know that speed, coordination, and strength were highly valued. These are, after all, the very foundation of warrior arts. Running is referred to often in the tales of the Fianna, referring to speed compared with horses or deer.(157) Running, both long-distance and sprinting, is also just a vital part of survival, and something that can only be developed through actual running. We can probably feel very traditional about it as long as we are outdoors and using a more natural mid-foot stride.(158) For strength, we may have to forgo tradition, as we have little to go on. Instead we use the variety of standard strength training methods we have available to us, some of which date back to the Greeks and Romans.(159) Certainly the basic concepts of progressive strength training by lifting objects and using body weight have been with humans of all cultures, while the methods may vary.(160) For tradition, some may wish to explore training for the heavy athletics of the Highland Games.

It is in martial arts training that the debate about tradition is strongest. We do have information and resources out there to consider traditional armed and unarmed Gaelic martial arts, some of which may be more modern, but are at least a part of the culture.(161) There are even organizations and groups that teach some of these styles, such as the Cateran Society, which offers Highland sword training.(162)

While I highly recommend participating in cultural arts, in some cases it may be difficult to train effectively and some methods may be too archaic to be useful. I believe that our actual fight training should be as practical as possible and include methods that work "on the streets." For many, especially those who are professional warriors such as law enforcement officers and soldiers, but also for many civilians, training would include modern firearms with defensive training. Self-defense training for both women and men is something I think should be considered, especially as many martial arts do not provide adequate street skills or do not give them quickly enough. I do not believe it is an either/or situation. Training as broadly as possible to include modern, nonculturally-related, and ancient culturally-related methods is the best option, as much as it may be possible. Given that we may not have the time or money for everything, I feel it is important to prioritize the practical and go from there, but the more you have in your arsenal, the better off you are.

I also believe that survival training, both wilderness and urban, is vital for someone on this path. Here we have only alluring hints of traditional Gaelic ways. Certainly we can connect this to the Outlaw Warbands who lived in the wildest places, but we instead must look at current training which should, at its best, not relate to any particular culture. This means avoiding the "survival schools" which mostly offer pseudo-Native practices and seeing those which actually offer survival training without appropriation. We should be best prepared for the wilderness or urban area(s) we are most likely to end up in, and from there have enough common-sense knowledge to guide us if we end up in a different location. It is also important to get guidance from someone who has experience and knowledge. Books are helpful, but they cannot replace a real-life teacher with a good background, and not someone with a few New-Age Pretindian seminars.(163) Foraging plants is a skill that should be part of long-term training. Not only can it be practiced legally, while survival-style hunting cannot, but plants are the most dangerous wild food and must be well known before they can be identified as edible.(164)

A further part of survival, of course, is preparation, which I believe is also a vital extension of the self- and communal-reliance that the warbands would have had. Preparedness for both short-term and long-term disasters might incorporate the survival and self-defense skills mentioned above, but also go-bags and food storage, whether traditional real food or MRIs.(165) Involvement in Community Emergency Response Teams (CERT) can help find your own plan and aid your community through various crises.(166)

This leads to an important consideration. Serving any Deity should include some sort of service to a community, even for those following a traditionally Outlaw path. The Fianna served the tribes, even while outside them. Therefore it is fitting for someone to honor their ties to the Morrígan by offering aid to the community. This can be in a professional capacity of law enforcement officer, firefighter, and/or soldier. However, I do not follow with the idea that to walk the warrior path we all end up becoming professional warriors. Therefore CERT is a way to offer that service in the local community, as for those so qualified doing things such as teaching self-defense, working with troubled kids, or many other options one might consider.

For many of us who are dedicated to *an Morrígan* or the other War Goddesses, we do not see this physical training as mundane. Many of us have developed personal ways to make our training – our sweat and tears – into dedications. We may recite prayers before, during, and after. We may make oaths that relate to our physical training. We may ask for help with reciprocation, asking to be made stronger and more skilled to better serve. I keep a shrine in the corner of my gym, and there will be some form of a shrine at our shooting range. I have many locations on our land where I might make offerings. Whether or not we practice magical or ecstatic arts, we tend to make our fitness and martial training a spiritual act: a dedication to Her.

XII: Who We Serve: Conclusion

Given the confusion we find in the texts, the possibility that we're dealing with several similar Goddesses and that the titles such as *an Morrígan* and Badb may have been used to signify any number of Them, we should consider that we, as actual worshipers, might not always know Who we are dealing with. There also is the possibility that we may be dealing with a variety of similar territorial Goddesses as I suggested, and many of us are not in any of those territories. We may even consider that when any two or more of us are talking about the War Goddess(es), we may not be talking about the same Ones, even if we are using the same names or titles. There is much vagueness, and sometimes it is very frustrating for us.

I believe this is due to our limitations and our weaknesses, not Theirs, and we should be careful to not assign too many limits to Them instead of seeing that it comes from ourselves. As a Polytheist, I also have no issue with seeing each as an individual and worshipping all, while at the same time knowing I might not always know with Whom I am dealing. I prefer to believe my Deities are complex, rather than archetypal and one-dimensional, and I like that They are difficult to categorize in these ways. Perhaps They do not always wish to be fully known. Perhaps we do not always need to know, because that's not the important part.

While not assigning limitations, note that while I found everything here pointed back to Them as War Goddesses, this doesn't mean that that is all They are. I hope I made that richness clear. The idea that we who serve this way see *an Morrígan* as just a War Goddess obviously suggests that the accuser sees a War Goddess as limited. I do not see the War Goddesses as just anything. They are expansive. To claim She is not a War Goddess at all, however, does limit Her, denies Her that role, and is often done in an attempt to deny that it is "inappropriate" for a female Deity. I do not see warfare as out of the reach of the feminine, or that we or our Goddesses must be limited by the idea that it is. Human women are mothers and warriors; why not our Goddesses?

It may be telling that although the early Christian Irish culture did not accept women as warriors,(167) they still showed Goddesses connected to war, as well as mentioning some female warriors in the literature. Some claim that this was to demonize Them,(168) that They are often terrifying and "demonic." This may be true; the idea probably was terrifying to the Christian writers. But I think They were included in spite of this, not in order to portray Them in a negative light but, I believe, because They demanded to be included and not made sweet and saintly. Being terrifying, being phantom, being a howler in the night is only a bad thing for those kept awake by such things. Not for the ones who are or who run with such things.

Endnotes

[1] Unsubstantiated Personal Gnosis is a term which apparently developed in the Norse Heathen community for what we might experience and believe that cannot be verified in the texts or archaeology. There is also Shared Personal Gnosis which is when others have come to the same knowledge independently. While there are some who look for prettier culturally relevant terms for these things, I have not yet decided what I would use and these are the terms which most readers will know.

[2] There are many resources in feminist analysis of such coding, but given the likely interests of my intended audience I will point out two feminist studies of portions of the Ulster Cycle which utilize this approach, Joanne Findon, *A Woman's Words: Emer and Female Speech in the Ulster Cycle*, Toronto: University of Toronto Press, 1997 and Diana Dominguez. *Historical Residues in the Old Irish Legends of Queen Medb: An Expanded Interpretation of the Ulster Cycle*, Lewiston, NY: The Edwin Mellen Press, 2010

[3] Dominguez, discuss this particularly in Ch. 2 of *Historical Residues...* but touches upon it throughout her study.

[4] Lisa M. Bitel in *Land of Women: Tales of Sex and Gender from Early Ireland*, Ithaca: Cornell University Press, 1996 pg. 13 notes that "...the literati disagreed about everything...." Really, why should it have been different then?

[5] An accessible run down of the nativist/anti-nativist and what's in between issues is Jonathan M. Wooding's "Reapproaching the Pagan Celtic Past – Anti-Nativism, Asterisk Reality and the Late-Antiquity Paradigm" *Studia Celtica Fennica VI*, Finnish Society for Celtic Studies, 2009 pg. 51-74

[6] Maya St.Clair, "*An Morrígan*: War Goddess and More"

[7] Whitley Stokes, trans. "The Second Battle of Moytura" Revue Celtique 12, pg. 128 also cited by Rosalind Clark. *The Great Queens: Irish Goddesses from the Morrigan to Cathleen ni*

Houlihan, Savage, MD: Barnes and Nobel Books, 1991 pg. 22 and Angelique Gulermovich Epstein, "War Goddess: the Morrígan and her Germano-Celtic Counterparts" dissertation for UCLA, 1998, Ch. 1 under heading "Etymologies" (formatting is messed up on my copy, as with those of everyone I know who has it, therefore the best I can offer for location is by chapter)

[8] Epstein Ch.1 notes "nightmare" Clark, pg 22 notes that this does not mean "female horse." There is no actual etymological connection between "mare" "specter" and "mare" "a female horse" for all that these Goddesses, especially Macha, do have a connection to horses. Paula Power Coe, "Macha and Conall Cernach: A Study of Two Iconographic Patterns in Medieval Irish Narratives and Celtic Art" UCLA dissertation 1995

[9] Stokes, trans. "The Second Battle of Moytura" pg. 128, Clark. *The Great Queens*, pg. 22 and Epstein.

[10] Máire Herbert, "Transmutations of an Irish Goddess" in Sandra Billington and Miranda Green, eds., *The Concept of the Goddess*, New York: Routledge, 1996 pg. 142

[11] Epstein, Ch. 1 section "Etymologies"

[12] *eDIL Letter*: M, Column: 166, Line: 057.

The woman's name "Mór" appears to have been quite popular in Medieval times, at least among the Uí Bhriain. This was noted by Muireann Ní Bhrolcháin in "The Banshenshas Revisited" in Mary O'Dowd and Sabine Wichert, eds., *Chattel, Servant or Citizen: Women's Status in Church, State and Society*, Belfast: The Institute of Irish Studies, The Queen's University of Belfast, 1995 pg. pg 75 n34. If it were a common name, then it might also account for it becoming a more popular spelling and meaning of the Goddess's title. Ní Bhrolcháin does also note that due to negative connotations of the adjective "large" for women now it's a name unlikely to become popular today. However, such names are still perhaps more rarely used today.

[13] Elizabeth Gray, trans. *Cath Maige Tuired: The Second Battle of Mag Tuired* Dublin: Irish Text Society, English para. 84, Irish pg. 44

Other features include "the Two Paps of the Morrígain" "Da Cích na Morrígna iarsain."(Whitley Stokes, ed. 'The Prose Tales in the Rennes Dindshenchas', *Revue Celtique* 15 (1894) English pg. 293 and Irish pg. 292).

[14] RAS MacAlister, ed. and trans., *Lebor Gabála Érenn: The Book of the Taking of Ireland Vol IV.* Dublin:Irish Text Society, 1941pg. 102, 298 Regarding the meanings of "mór" I also thank Caera Aislingeach for private correspondence on the word.

[15] Epstein. Kim Heijda, "War-goddesses, furies and scald crows: The use of the word badb in early Irish literature" thesis, University of Utrecht, Feb. 27, 2007 pg. 9-18, but, also in more detail in sections titled according to meaning.

[16] MacAlister, *Lebor Gabála Érenn*, WM Hennessey. "The Ancient Irish Goddess of War" *Revue Celtique vol 1.* 1870 pg. 32-57 , Proinsias MacCana. *Celtic Mythology*, NY: Peter Bedrick Books, 1987, pg. 86-88, Miranda Green, *Celtic Goddesses: Warriors, Virgins and Mothers.* New York: George Braziller, pg. 41-42, Clark pg. 39-40 for example

[17] Hennessey pg. 34

[18] Heijda, pg. 32

[19] I am refraining from pointing to such sources, they are easy to find on the internet, however. For an examination of Grave's M/M/C concept see Ronald Hutton, *The Pagan Religions of the Ancient British Isles: Their Nature and Legacy*, Cambridge, MA: Blackwell Publishers, Inc., 1995 pg. 145, 153, 326, 335

[20] Cecile O'Rahilly, trans. *Táin Bó Cúalnge, Recession 1* Dublin: Dublin Institute for Advanced Studies, 1976 English, Irish or see Thomas Kinsella, trans. The Tain: from the Irish epic *Tain Bo Cuailnge.* Oxford: Oxford University Press, 1969

[21] Niall: Tom Peete Cross and Clark Harris Slover, eds., "The Adventures of the Sons of Eochaid Mugmedon," *Ancient Irish Tales* New York: Barns & Noble, 1996 pg. 508-513. Macha: John O'Donovan ed. and trans., Annala Rioghachta Eireann: *Annals of the Kingdom of Ireland by the Four Masters, from the earliest period to the year 1616.* Library of the Royal Irish Academy and of Trinity College Dublin Pt 1 M4505-M4546 English, Irish

[22] Georges Dumézil, *"Le trio des Macha"* Revue de l'histoire des religions 146, 6 1954. pg. 5-17 He used only the three, of five Machas found in the texts, noted in the Dindshenchas (place name stories) for Ard Macha, the wife of Nemed he labeled sacral/sovereign, Macha Mongruadh as warrior and the pregnant, horse racing Macha ingen Sainrith meic Inboith as fertility/production. This leaves out the actual Goddess we're discussing here, as it's unknown if any of these particular Machas were ever considered Goddesses. See for example of their stories: Edward Gwynn, ed. *The Metrical Dindshenchas Vol. 4*, Dublin: Dublin Institute for Advanced Studies, 1991 (org. 1906) English Irish Poem 12 or Whitley Stokes *The Prose Tales in the Rennes Dindshenchas*, 94 Ard Macha English, Irish

[23] John Carey, "Notes on the Irish War Goddess" *Éigse*, Vol. 19, 1980-1981, pg. 263-275

[24] LGÉ IV

[25] As the genitive "Anann" can be used as a nomitive, I shall be using this rather than the more familiar "Anu." This is in part due to it reading better for me in connotation with Buanann.

[26] LGÉ IV pg. 103 for MacAlister's noting this being "true name." listings at pg.130-131, 160-161, 188-189, Heijda pg. 34, Epstein Ch. 1

[27] LGÉ IV pg. 122-123, 130-131,154-155, 160-161, 182-183, 216-217

[28] LGÉ IV, pg. 103 n5, 310

[29] Heijda, pg. 33

[30] Gray CMT English para. 166, Irish pg. 70 or Stokes, "The Second Battle of Moytura" pg. 110-111

[31] Kuno Meyer, trans. 'The Wooing of Emer'"Tochmarc Emire," *Archaeological Review 1*, 1888, English Irish para 50

[32] Heijda pg. 33

[33] Heijda pg. 36-38

[34] While there is the other triple sisterhood of daughters of Ernmas (Ériu, Fotla and Banba) for convenience I will be using this term when speaking of her daughters, Badb, Macha, Anann/Morrígan collectively for this paper.

[35] Again see MacCana, *Celtic Mythology*, pg. 86, Green, *Celtic Goddesses*, pg. 41-42., also Bitel, *Land of Women*, pg. 208 for example

[36] Hennessey, pg. 33, 34

[37] Green, *Celtic Goddesses*, pg. 41-42 She actually lists these names as: "Morrigán, Macha, Badb, and Nemain" while saying they are three, then soon immediately drops "Macha" to again list the other three. (this accent, on the "a" but not the "i" or the "o," appears to be peculiar to Green and some who follow her work)

[38] As Green does in *Celtic Goddesses* pg. 42 as noted above

[39] LGÉ IV pg. 130-131, 194-195, it's the one on pg. 188-189 which includes Elcmar as Ernmas' son (although, of course, that doesn't mean that They couldn't be sisters as well, as we see incest in many of these genealogies, if they were also listed as Ernmas' daughters)

[40] LGÉ IV pg. 154-155, 160-161, 188-189, 236-237. Epstein. John O'Donovan, ed. and trans. (with notes and translations from Whitley Stokes) Sanas Cormaic Calcutta: O. T. Cutter for the Irish Archeological and Celtic Society, 1868, pg. 26 122

[41] Clark, pg. 39

[42] Heijda pg. 40

[43] Epstein Ch 1, Heijda pg. 43

[44] LGÉ IV pg. 188, 189

[45] Meyer, "Tochmarc Emire" English Irish para 50"H-i Ross Bodbo .i. na Morrighno, ar iss ed a ross-side Crich Roiss & iss i an bodb catha h-i & is fria id-beurur bee Neid .i. bandee in catæ, uair is inann be Neid & dia cathæ"

[46] Again, NeoPagan sources, Google…."Morrighan" and "Hennessey" should get you there. Epstein does, however, also note that Hennessey may indeed the first modern scholar to call Her a War Goddess, a credit which may have confused some people.

[47] *The Metrical Dindshenchas Vol. 4* Poem 49 English Irish "Moch dia m-boí 'na codlud Odras groc-dub gnóach, dosrocht ben in Dagda, ba samla día sóach."

[48] Stokes, "The Prose Tales…" English, Irish pg. 62

[49] Hennessey pg. 32-57

[50] Although Hutton has suggested exactly that regarding Macha in *The Pagan Religions of the Ancient British Isles* pg. 154 "It looks as if the authors knew nothing of her except her name, and were inventing stories to go with it." This may have been true, given that none of the Machas in the Dindshenchas match the daughter of Ernmas, however it seems more likely that the stories existed, whether attached to such a name or not.

[51] Máire Herbert, "Transmutations of an Irish Goddess" pg. 148 is at the forefront of blaming the Christian theologians. Mary Condren in *The Serpent* and *The Goddess: Women, Religion and Power in Celtic Ireland*. San Francisco: HarperSanFrancisco, 1989 promotes the concept a pre-Celtic peaceful Great Mother Goddess, who she says was Macha in Ireland, being usurped by the "patriarchal hordes" of the Celts and turned the Loving Mother into a War Goddess Who only attacked male warriors rather than help any of them. This is throughout the book, but prominent on pg. 35

I'm not going to offer any NeoPagan citations, they are growing and you can Google it for yourself. The spelling "Morrighan" seems to be more popular so you might want to use that one.

[52] Marie-Louise Sjoestedt, *Celtic Gods and Heroes*, New York: Dover Publications, Inc., Mineola 2000, pg. 18-19
[53] Carey, "Notes on the Irish War Goddess," pg. 263-268, especially, but through to 275
[54] For the concepts in early Ireland see Bitel, *Land of Women*
[55] For example: Clark pg. 29-32, Green pg. 45, Herbert pg. 144-145,
[56] Nerys Patterson. *Cattle Lords & Clansmen: The Social Structure of Early Ireland*, Notre Dame, IN: University of Notre Dame, 1994 pg. 133-134 and elsewhere, Barry Raftery. *Pagan Celtic Ireland: the Enigma of the Irish Iron Age*, New York: Thames & Hudson, 1994, pg. 125
[57] Epstein Intro, Ch. 1
[58] A. H. Leahy, ed. and trans, "Táin Bó Regamna," *Leahy Heroic Romances of Ireland, Volume II* London: David Nutt, 1906 English, Irish
[59] Kuno Meyer, *Echtrae Nerai* (The Adventure of Nera) *Revue celtique* 10 (1889), pg. 212-228, the "Pillow Talk" is of course, gives her motive, as well as the long standing feud with her former husband Conchobar of Ulster, who had raped her and killed her husband in Joseph O'Neill, ed. & trans., "Cath Boinde", *Ériu* 2, 1905, pp. 173-185 as well as killing her son A. H. Leahy, *The Courtship of Ferb: An Old Irish Romance* Transcribed in the 12th Century into the *Book of Leinster*, New York, 1902. Needless to say her anger wasn't as "unreasonable" or "trivial" as sometimes gets made out. See *Historical Residues in the Old Irish Legends of Queen Medb: An Expanded Interpretation of the Ulster Cycle*, Lewiston, NY: The Edwin Mellen Press, 2010 for a detailed study of Medb. Also see Epstein for commentary regarding the connection of these tales with the Morrígan's connection to warfare.
[60] *The Metrical Dindshenchas Vol. 4* English, Irish Poem 49. Whitley Stokes, trans., "The Prose Tales…", English pg. 65, Irish

pg. 64-65, Whitley Stokes, trans, "The Bodleian Dinnshenchas" *Folklore, Vol. 3*, No. 4, Dec., 1892 English, Irish pg. 471

[61] Ibid.

[62] Stokes, "The Prose Tales…" English, Irish pg. 62, "The Bodleian Dinnshenchas" English, Irish pg. 471

[63] CMT English para. 84, Irish pg. 44.

[64] *Táin Bó Cúalnge Recession 1* English pg. 177, Irish pg. 57

[65] *Macha: Annals of the Four Masters Pt 1* M4505-M4546 English, Irish *The Metrical Dindshenchas Vol. 4* English Irish Poem 12, Keating, *The History of Ireland Vol. 2* English Irish Section 28 and Meyer, *The Wooing Of Emer* English Irish para. 30, Niall "The Adventures of the Sons of Eochaid Mugmedon"

[66] Herbert, "Transmutations of an Irish Goddess" pg. 143

[67] Proinsias Mac Cana. *Celtic Mythology*, NY: Peter Bedrick Books, 1987 pg. 92-93, see also Clark, pg. 109-185. Also see Bart Jaski. *Early Irish Kingship and Succession*. Dublin: Four Courts Press, 2000, for a look at questioning of how and when it might have been practiced in actuality.

[68] Stokes 'The Prose Tales in the Rennes Dindshenchas' English pg. 293 Irish pg. 292

[69] These claims largely come from the NeoPagan community and I will leave it up to you to find them as I simply do not wish to have certain links here.

[70] And that we do not have a consensus of what they were. See Donald MacKinnon, "Fulacht na Morrigna" *The Celtic Review, vol. 8*, 1912 74-76 ft , Douglas Hyde, "Cooking of the Great Queen (Fulacht na Morrigna)" *The Celtic Review vol. 10* ,1916 pg 335-351, Keating, *The History of Ireland, Vol. 3* English Irish Section 30, Peter Harbison. *Pre-Christian Ireland: From the First Settlers to the Early Celts*, New York: Thames & Hudson, 1988 pg. 110-111, Hennessey pg. 54-55, "Ancient monument may have been Bronze Age Brewery," DA Ó Drisceoil, "Burnt Mounds: cooking or bathing?," *Antiquity*,

1988, Vol. 62 and "Fulachta Fiadh – An Irish Mystery" by Anne-Maire Denvir

[71] *LGÉ IV* pg. 128, 129

[72] John Carey. "The Name 'Tuatha Dé Danann'" *Éigse*, Vol. 18, 1980-1981, pg. 291 it should also be noted that this title of Gods shifts, as does Their parentage to a degree that just can't be covered here.

[73] *LGÉ IV* pg. 188, 189 "In Mor-rigu, ingen Delbaith mathair an mac aile Dealbaith .i. Brian 7 Iucharba 7 Iuchair: 7 is dia forainm Danand o builead Da Chich Anan for Luachair, 7 o builed Tuatha De Danann"

[74] *LGÉ IV* pg. 182, 183 "Badbh 7 Macha 7 Morrighan 7 Anand, diata di chich Anand i l-Luaehair, tri hingeana Earnmhais na ban-thuathaighe, 7 is i in Danand sin mathair na ndee, i is iad a hingena, .i. Airgdean i Barrand i Be Chuille 1 Be Thedhe"

[75] O'Donovan, ed. and trans. (Stokes) *Sanas Cormaic* pg.4 see also Epstein, Ch 1

[76] J. Fraser "The First Battle of Moytura." *Ériu 8*, 1915, para 29, 48, (English translation only)

[77] CMT, English para. 106-119 Irish pg 52, 54

[78] Epstein, Ch 1 "Badb bean in Dagda Mor. Anand .i. in Mor-rigan (diata Da Chich Anand for Luachair Deadad,) bean aile don Dagda"

[79] Epstein, Ch 1 "De 7 Danand in da ban-de diatat Tuatha De 7 Danand, (7 nidad inand 7 in rigraig dia mbai in Dagda Mor 7 Lug et rel.) da mnai Tuireand"

[80] Carey, "The Name 'Tuatha Dé Danann.', pg. 291-94, and Alexei Kondratiev, "Danu and Bile: The Primordial Parents?" *An Tríbhís Mhór: The IMBAS Journal of Celtic Reconstructionism Vol. 1*, No. 4, Bealtaine 1998 Both Carey and Kondratiev suggest the use of the reconstructed form, with the asterisk, as the name "Danu" never appears in the actual Irish texts.

[81] *LGÉ IV* pg. 188, 189

[82] See Bitel pg. 86 for discussion of how these terms are translated in regards to the position of "mother" in early Christian Ireland. The more affectionate "muimme" appears to have been reserved for foster-mother not biological mother.

[83] O'Donovan, *Sanas Cormaic* pg. 17   He included this note: "It is impossible to bring buan 'good' from the Latin bonum with its short penult. Rather cf. W.buan 'swifV, which seems the Skr. javana. For the change of meaning from ' swift' to ' good' cf. cnrovlaioς. As to Buanann, I would connect it with the Skr. bhdvana ' auctor , * creator'. — Ed."

The Irish is:

Buanand muimme nafiann .i. be nAnand [ar] cosmaile diblínib.
amail robu máthair dee indí Ánu sic Buanand erat máthair
nafian .i. dagmathair. [Aliter Buanand] am buan .i. is bón
.i. dendi is bonum. amail dicitur genither buan o ambuan
.i. maith o ulc. an and fil isinní is Buanand (is mater) is
[ed fil] inni is Anu .i. mater deorum. Buanand din .i. dághmathair

ocforcedul gaiscid donafianaib.

Whitley Stokes, ed., 'Cormac's Glossary' in Three Irish Glossaries, London: Williams and Norgate, 1862 pg. 6

[84] Stokes 'The Prose Tales in the Rennes Dindshenchas' English Irish

[85] Those that mention Macha's death include Whitley Stokes *The Prose Tales in the Rennes Dindshenchas*, 94 Ard Macha English, Irish and Stokes, "The Edinburgh Dinnshenchas" Folklore 4 (1893) 480-481 English, Irish. Others such as *The Metrical Dindshenchas Vol. 4* English Irish Poem 12 mention nothing of Her death. Although modern tellings often include the twins dying as well, and this is how I first learned the story through oral telling, I have not found an actual version that gives this, let alone any that tell of Her stomping off with them under Her arms back to the Otherworld, as is even more popular these days.

[86] Epstein

[87] "clann na Morrigna ingine Ernnmais, cona seisser ar .xx. ban-gaiscedach, 7 cona seisser ar .xx. fer-gaiscedach" Whitley Stokes, ed. *Acallamh na Senórach I* Stokes & E. Windisch, ed., Irische Texte vol. 4 part 1, 1900, pg. 140 translation is from Epstein Ch. 3., also Standish Hayes O'Grady, trans. "The Colloquy of the Ancients" Medieval Irish Series, Cambridge, 1999 which includes only the 26 "she-warriors" but leaves out the 26 male warriors. Pg 128

[88] Epstein Ch. 3

[89] Fraser "The First Battle of Moytura." para 20

[90] CMT Gray English para. 118-119, Irish pg. 54

[91] Bitel, *Land of Women*, pg. 216

[92] Fraser "The First Battle of Moytura." para. 29, 48

[93] CMT English para. 106-119, Irish pg. 52, 54

[94] CMT English para. 137, Irish pg.

[95] Or, rather, begins to. The entirety has not been translated nor typically even transcribed. A friend looking for a digital copy of the manuscript has noted that the page is, in fact, missing. So where this dire prediction might have gone after the few lines, if perhaps things resolved or not, is unknown. CMT Gray English para. 166-167, Irish pg. 170, 172

[96] CMT English para. 85, Irish pg. 44 Epstein argues that this knowledge may not be Sight but "inside information" as there are connections between *an Morrígan* and the Fomoire, which is not only too complex to explore here, but also hardly unique among the Tuatha Dé Danann, many of whom have Fomoire blood or are intermarried, so see Epstein Ch 1

[97] Cecile O'Rahilly, trans., *Táin Bó Cúalnge from Book of Leinster Dublin*: Dublin Institute for Advanced Studies, 1967 English pg. 174, Irish pg. 35-36, see also TBC Rec 1 English pg. 152, Irish pg. 30.

[98] *Táin Bó Regamna* English, Irish

[99] Nagy. The Wisdom of the Outlaw pg. 102

[100] *Tochmarc Emire* English, Irish para.70-71, 78-79   Also see Nora Chadwick, "Imbas Forosnai" *Scottish Gaelic Studies, vol 4*, part 2, Oxford University Press, 1935

[101] Here we see the use of badb as "witch" but perhaps particularly a war-witch, see Heijda's work on the meaning of "badb" especially Chps. 4.2

[102] E. Curry, ed & tr, *Cath Mhuighe Léana* or *The Battle of Mag Léana* together with *Tochmarc* Moméra or the Courtship of Moméra Dublin: 1855 pg. 32, 33

[103] Joseph Falaky Nagy. *The Wisdom of the Outlaw: The Boyhood Deeds of Finn in Gaelic Narrative Tradition*, Berkeley: University of California Press, 1985, also Hilda Ellis Davidson, "The Seer's Thumb" in Davidson, ed., *The Seer in Celtic and Other Traditions*, Edinburgh: John Donald Publishers LTD, 1989 pg. 66-78. Chadwick, "Imbas Forosnai". A comprehensive catalogue of all mentions in the tales would be impossible for me in this footnote

[104] Phillip A. Bernhardt-House, "Warriors, Words, and Wood: Oral and Literary Wisdom in the Exploits of Irish Mythological Warriors" *Studia Celtica Fennica VI*,   Finnish Society for Celtic Studies, 2009 pg. 5-19

[105] There are many who have claimed this, such as Bitel and Clark who have been mentioned elsewhere. It is one of the areas where personal coding, personal bias, seems to clearly get in the way, and slight evidence is extrapolated into complete "fact" in order to fit certain worldviews. A prime example would be Michael J. Enright, who in his *Lady with the Mead Cup: Ritual, Prophecy and Lordship in the European Warband from La Tène to the Viking Age*, Portland, OR: Four Courts Press, 2007 ignores the warrior-seers completely in Ch. V on Celtic warbands to "support" his insistence that the only role for women in the bands was as prophetesses and arbitrators then goes into a strange, unsubstantiated "evidence" in a long footnote on how physically impossible it is for women to fight on page 211. I recommend Colette Dowling. *The Frailty Myth:*

Redefining the Physical Potential of Women and Girls, New York: Random House, 2001 as just one text on why his argument doesn't hold.

[106] Epstein, Ch 1

[107] TBC Rec 1 English pg. 180-181, Irish pg. 61-62 and TBC from *Book of Leinster* English pg. 194-195, Irish pg. 54-55

[108] *Macha: Annals of the Four Masters Pt 1* M4505-M4546 English, Irish see also *The Metrical Dindshenchas Vol. 4* English Irish Poem 12, Keating, The History of Ireland Vol. 2 English Irish Section 28 and *The Wooing Of Emer* English, Irish para. 30

[109] CMT English para. 133, Irish pg. 60

[110] MacAlister, LGE IV, pg. 236-237

[111] Fraser "The First Battle of Moytura." para 29, para. 48

[112] TBC Rec 1 English pg. 231, 234, Irish pg. 118, 121

[113] Epstein

[114] Matthias Egeler, "Death, Wings, and Divine Devouring: Possible Mediterranean Affinities of Irish Battlefield Demons and Norse Valkyries" *Studia Celtica Fennica V*, Finnish Society for Celtic Studies, 2008 pg. 5-26

[115] Epstein, Heijda

[116] AG van Hamel Compert Con *Culainn and Other Stories, Medieval and Modern Irish Series, Vol 3*, Dublin: Dublin Institute for Advanced Studies, 1933, for the Irish. 69-133. Hayes O'Grady, trans., "The Great Defeat on the Plain of Muirthemne before Cuchullin's Death" and Whitley Stokes, trans., "The Tragical Death of Cochulainn," both in Eleanor Hull, ed., *The Cuchullin Saga in Irish Literature: being a collection of stories relating to the Hero Cuchullin*, London: David Nutt on the Strand, 1898, pg. 235-263 for translation

[117] Epstein. pg. Ch. 2, from van Hamel Irish pg. 96, O'Grady, English pg. 247

[118] Epstein Ch. 2, and elsewhere tries to sort through this, Heijda, Ch. 4.2

[119] Epstein, Ch. 2, Heijda, pg. 62

[120] TBC BoL English pg. 149, Irish pg. 13

[121] Patricia Lysaght, "Aspects of the Earth-Goddess in the Traditions of the Banshee in Ireland" Billington and Green, eds., *The Concept of the Goddess*

[122] J. Fraser "The First Battle of Moytura." para 48

[123] Findon. *A Woman's Words*, pg 58, it is noted, that, this conflict is a reflection of the male conflict as well. In the tales we see males primarily united when at war with others, but in competition when not…after all, conflict turns stories. But it's rarer to see such camaraderie among women in any of the tales. The noble women do have retinues, but these other women are largely invisible and silent, serving only to enhance the primary woman in some way, as with Emer in *Tochmarc Emire*, as noted in Bitel, *Land of Women*, pg. 145-146, there really is no interaction. Bitel notes that women do not bond in warfare as the men do. In *Serglige Con Culainn* (The Wasting Sickness of Cú Chulainn), we again hear of Emer leading her retinue of women into a sort of battle against her husband's Otherworldly lover Fand, but, again, other than that mention, there is no actual relating between her and the women and, of course, this aspect of the story is about the conflict between two women over a man and actually allows a voice mocking women going to war with Cú Chulainn's rebuke of Emer. See also Findon, *A Woman's Words*. Ch. 4 especially pg. 108-109, 120, 124

[124] A. H. Leahy, *The Courtship of Ferb*

[125] Ibid. Heijda goes into the variations in more detail.

[126] Leahy

[127] Again, see Dominguez for discussion on Medb

[128] For example, Sjoestedt pg.26

[129] For example, Clark pg. 12, 28

[130] Green does so somewhat in "Celtic Goddesses" on pg. 140, although on 149 she also puts her in the Otherworld

[131] Nagy, Wisdom of the Outlaw, pg. 102 and 265 n13, Epstein, Ch. 2, TBC from BoL English pg. 231 (leaves out "búanand"), Irish pg. 95

[132] Nagy notes Scáthach's name meaning "reflection" and "shadow" in connection to Cú Chulainn and her other students being reflections of her and her a shadow of them in *Conversing with Angels and Ancient: Literary Myths of Medieval Ireland*. Ithaca: Cornell University Press, 1997, pg. 220

[133] Nagy Wisdom of the Outlaw, pg. 102, Epstein Ch.

[134] Epstein, Ch

[135] Green again notes possible "priestess" status for Finn's foster-mothers in Celtic Goddesses pg. 140

[136] Epstein, Ch. 3 prior to conclusions

[137] Kim McCone notes that Sjoestadt's (and others) assertion that there is a clear distinction between "hero within the tribe" (exemplified by CC) and "hero outside of the tribe" (exemplified by Finn) is probably a false distinction which he attributes to monastic manipulation. "Werewolves, Cyclopes, Díberga and Fíanna: Juvenile Delinquency in Early Ireland" *Cambridge Medieval Celtic Studies,* issue 12, 1986, pg. 8. This is a concept I have been working on examining in something related to this article.

[138] Not surprisingly, Herbert primarily dismisses their contentious interactions as the Christian transcribers demonizing *an Morrígan.* pg. 146-148 while we've already mentioned that Condren seems to believe the War Goddesses always work against the warriors, apparently regardless of which side of the battle, pg. 35, Clark likewise notes that She is angered by him but his rage does not last, yet she does also note the

[139] Epstein, pg. 134

[140] TBC Rec 1 English pg. 139, Irish pg. 16 See also Epstein Ch. 2

[141] Epstein following Proinsias MacCana in "Láided, Gressacht 'Formalized Incitement'" Érui vol. 43 pg. 69-92

[142] TBC Rec 1 English pg. 207, Irish pg. 93 and TBC BoL English pg. 227, Irish pg. 90

[143] TBC Rec 1 English pg. 180-181, Irish pg. 61-62 and TBC BoL English pg. 194-195, Irish pg. 54-55

[144] TBC Rec 1 English pg. 177, Irish pg. 57

[145] TBC Rec 1 English pg. 180-182, Irish pg. 61-63 and TBC BoL English pg. 194-197, Irish pg. 54-57

[146] TBC Rec 1 English pg. 137, 147-148, 171, Irish pg. 14, 25-26, 51 and TBC BoL English pg. 170-171, 201-202, Irish pg. 32-33, 61-62

[147] Epstein

[148] Kim McCone, "Werewolves, …." 1986, Máire West, "Aspects of díberg in the tale Togail Bruidne Da Derga" *Zeitschrift für celtische Philologie* (ZcP) , *Volume 49-50*, 1997

[149] TBC Rec 1 English pg. 189, Irish pg. 71 and TBC BoL English pg. 204, Irish pg. 64

[150] This latter is the subject of Peter Schrijver, "Henbane and early European narcotics" *Zeitschrift für celtische Philologie* (ZcP) , *Volume 51*, 1999

[151] McCone, "Werewolves, Cyclopes,…"

[152] O'Grady "Colloquy of the Ancients" Stokes, ed. *Acallamh na Senórach I* Irish.

[153] McCone, "Werewolves, Cyclopes,…" also Nagy, Wisdom of the Outlaw, pg 20-21, 49-50, 139 and elsewhere through the book

[154] Chadwick, "Imbas Forosnai"

[155] Davidson, "The Seer's Thumb" 66-78

[156] Another CR view, from someone who can articulate his experience a bit more than I seem able at this time, of fáelad can be found in various posts at A Wolf-Man, Not a Wolf in Man's Clothing

[157] Nagy, *Wisdom of the Outlaw*, pg. 51,95-96, 104-105, 135, 176

[158] Danny Abshire and Brian Metzler *Natural Running: The Simple Path to Stronger, Healthier Running* Boulder Colorado: Velopress, 2010 and Danny and Kathryn Dreyer, *Chi Running: A Revolutionary Approach to Effortless, Injury-free Running*, New

York: Fireside – Simon & Schuster, 2004 The authors' connection of this with the Chinese concept of Chi may kill the "we're oh so traditional" joke a little, but it remains a good resource for relearning a more natural method of running.

[159] Jan Todd, Ph.D. "From Milo to Milo: A History of Barbells, Dumbells, and Indian Clubs" *Iron Game History*, Vol. 3, No. 6, April 1995

[160] If I might be forgiven for citing my own work, I am doing a series on fitness for a secular physical feminist group centered around a modern woman warrior (although nothing I offer, aside from some indication that women do not, in fact, need to train differently than men, is gender specific) which can be found in The Sarah Connor Charm School Blog under "fitness."

[161] C. Lee Vermeers "Celtic Martial Arts"

[162] Cateran Society

[163] Tim Smith, "Real Bushcraft And Survival Training Has Nothing To Do With New Age Religion Or Misappropriating Native American Spirituality" While books alone are not adequate for training, John "Lofty" Wiseman, *SAS Survival Handbook: For Any Climate, In Any Situation* (revised edition), New York: Collins, 2009 is a good resource for basics..

[164] This is certainly where you do not want to depend on books, but they do help and a great start is with Samuel Thayer's *The Forager's Harvest: A Guide to Identifying, Harvesting, and Preparing Edible Wild Plants*, Birchwood, WI: Forager's Harvest Press, 2006 and *Nature's Garden: A Guide to Identifying, Harvesting, and Preparing Edible Wild Plants*, Birchwood, WI: Forager's Harvest Press, 2010. He also has DVDs. Get to know a plant real well before eating it, there are many innocent looking but deadly plants. Seek out knowledgeable and trust worthy mentors if possible. Do not eat a plant you are not 100% sure of.

[165] Jim MacDonald's "Jump Kits" page is a great guide

[166] Community Emergency Response Team (CERT) Program

[167] Bitel, Land of *Women*
[168] Herbert and Condren as noted earlier

Bibliography

Danny Abshire and Brian Metzler. *Natural Running: The Simple Path to Stronger, Healthier Running* (Boulder Colorado: Velopress, 2010

Lisa Bitel. *Land of Women: Tales of Sex and Gender from Early Ireland*, Ithaca: Cornell University Press, 1996

Phillip A. Bernhardt-House, "Warriors, Words, and Wood: Oral and Literary Wisdom in the Exploits of Irish Mythological Warriors" *Studia Celtica Fennica VI*, Finnish Society for Celtic Studies, 2009 pg. 5-19 http://www.sfks.org/Julkaisut.htm

Breakingnews.ie (no byline) "Ancient monument may have been Bronze Age Brewery"
http://www.breakingnews.ie/ireland/mhcwcwsnsncw/

John Carey. "The Name 'Tuatha Dé Danann'" *Éigse, Vol. 18*, prt. 2, pg. 291-94

------"Notes on the Irish War-Goddess" *Éigse, Vol. 19*, prt. 2, pg. 263-275

The Cateran Society http://www.cateransociety.com/

Nora Chadwick, "Imbas Forosnai" Scottish Gaelic Studies, vol 4, part 2, Oxford University Press, 1935

Rosalind Clark. *The Great Queens: Irish Goddesses from The Morrigan to Cathleen ni Houlihan*, Savage, MD: Barnes and Nobel Books, 1991

Paula Power Coe, "Macha and Conall Cernach: A Study of Two Iconographic Patterns in Medieval Irish Narratives and Celtic Art" UCLA dissertation, 1995

Community Emergency Response Team (CERT) Program website

http://www.citizencorps.gov/cert/index.shtm

Mary Condren, *The Serpent and The Goddess: Women, Religion and Power in Celtic Ireland*. San Francisco: HarperSanFrancisco, 1989

Tom Peete Cross and Clark Harris Slover, eds., "The Adventures of the Sons of Eochaid Mugmedon," *Ancient Irish Tales* New York: Barns & Noble, 1996 pg. 508-513 http://www.maryjones.us/ctexts/eochaid.html

E. Curry, ed & tr, *Cath Mhuighe Léana* or *The Battle of Mag Léana* together with *Tochmarc Moméra* or the *Courtship of Moméra* Dublin: 1855

http://archive.org/details/cathmhuighelana00ocugoog from the Irish

http://www.ucc.ie/celt/online/G302025/index.html

Hilda Ellis Davidson, "The Seer's Thumb," Davidson (ed.) *The Seer in Celtic and Other Traditions*, Edinburgh: John Donald Publishers LTD, 1989

Anne-Maire Denvir "Fulachta Fiadh – An Irish Mystery" http://www.angelfire.com/fl/burntmounds/

Diana Dominguez. *Historical Residues in the Old Irish Legends of Queen Medb: An Expanded Interpretation of the Ulster Cycle*, Lewiston, NY: The Edwin Mellen Press, 2010

Colette Dowling. *The Frailty Myth: Redefining the Physical Potential of Women and Girls*, New York: Random House, 2001

Danny and Kathryn Dreyer, *Chi Running: A Revolutionary Approach to Effortless, Injury-free Running*, New York: Fireside – Simon & Schuster, 2004

Georges Dumézil, "Le trio des Macha" *Revue de l'histoire des religions*, 146, 6 1954. pg. 5-17 http://www.persee.fr/web/revues/home/prescript/article/rhr_0035-1423_1954_num_146_1_6992

Matthias Egeler, "Death, Wings, and Divine Devouring: Possible Mediterranean Affinities of Irish Battlefield Demons and Norse Valkyries" *Studia Celtica Fennica V*, Finnish Society for Celtic Studies, 2008 http://www.sfks.org/Julkaisut.htm

Michael J. Enright, *Lady with the Mead Cup: Ritual, Prophecy and Lordship in the European Warband from La Tène to the Viking Age*, Portland, OR: Four Courts Press, 2007

Angelique Gulermovich Epstein, "War Goddess: The Morrígan and her Germano-Celtic Counterparts" dissertation, University of California in Los Angeles, 1998

J. Fraser "The First Battle of Moytura." *Ériu 8*, (1915) English translation can be found at: http://www.maryjones.us/ctexts/1maghtured.html

Eilzabeth Gray, trans. *Cath Maige Tuired: The Second Battle of Mag Tuired* Dublin: Irish Text Society, http://www.sacred-texts.com/neu/cmt/cmteng.htm from the Irish http://www.ucc.ie/celt/published/G300010/index.html

Miranda Green, *Celtic Goddesses: Warriors, Virgins and Mothers*. New York: George Braziller, 1996

Edward Gwynn, ed. *The Metrical Dindshenchas Vol. 4*, Dublin: Dublin Institute for Advanced Studies, 1991 (org. 1906) http://www.ucc.ie/celt/published/T106500D/ English, http://www.ucc.ie/celt/published/G106500D/ Irish

Peter Harbison. *Pre-Christian Ireland: From the First Settlers to the Early Celts*, New York: Thames & Hudson, 1988

Kim Heijda, "War-goddesses, furies and scald crows: The use of the word badb in early Irish literature" thesis, University of Utrecht, Feb. 27, 2007 http://igitur-archive.library.uu.nl/student-theses/2007-0620-200703/UUindex.html

WM Hennessey. "The Ancient Irish Goddess of War" *Revue Celtique vol 1*. 1870 pg. 32-57
http://www.archive.org/details/revueceltique01gaid

Máire Herbert, "Transmutations of an Irish Goddess" Miranda Green and Sandra Billington, eds., *The Concept of the Goddess*, New York: Routledge, 1996

Ronald Hutton, *The Pagan Religions of the Ancient British Isles: Their Nature and Legacy*, Cambridge, MA: Blackwell Publishers, Inc., 1995

Douglas Hyde, "Cooking of the Great Queen (Fulacht na Morrigna)" *The Celtic Review vol. 10*, 1916
http://www.archive.org/details/celticreview10edinuoft

Bart Jaski. *Early Irish Kingship and Succession*. Dublin: Four Courts Press, 2000

Geoffrey Keating (Seathrún Céitinn), *Foras Feasa ar Éirinn: The History of Ireland*, David Comyn, Patrick S. Dinneen, eds., London: David Nutt, for the Irish Texts Society, 1902–1914 Vol. 2
http://www.ucc.ie/celt/published/T100054/index.html English,
http://www.ucc.ie/celt/published/G100054/index.html Irish,
Vol. 3 http://www.ucc.ie/celt/published/T100054/index.html English,
http://www.ucc.ie/celt/published/G100054/index.html Irish

Thomas Kinsella, trans. The Tain: from the Irish epic *Tain Bo Cuailnge*. Oxford: Oxford University Press, 1969

Alexei Kondratiev, "Danu and Bile: The Primordial Parents?" *An Tríbhís Mhór: The IMBAS Journal of Celtic Reconstructionism Vol. 1, No. 4*, Bealtaine 1998
http://www.mythicalireland.com/mythology/tuathade/danubile.html

A. H. Leahy, *The Courtship of Ferb: An Old Irish Romance* Transcribed in the 12th Century into the *Book of Leinster*, New York 1902
http://www.maryjones.us/ctexts/ferb1.html English

------ ed. and trans, "Táin Bó Regamna," and *The Wasting Sickness of Cú Chulainn* (Serglige Con Culainn) Leahy, ed. *Heroic Romances of Ireland, Volume II* London: David Nutt, 1906 TBR
http://www.maryjones.us/ctexts/regamna.html English from
http://www.ucc.ie/celt/online/G301005/index.html Irish SCC
http://www.luminarium.org/mythology/ireland/cuchulainnsick.htm English from

http://www.ucc.ie/celt/published/G301015/index.html Irish

Patricia Lysaght, "Aspects of the Earth-Goddess in the Traditions of the Banshee in Ireland" Miranda Green and Sandra Billington, eds., *The Concept of the Goddess*, New York: Routledge, 1996

Robert A. Stewart MacAlister, ed. and trans., *Lebor Gabála Érenn: The Book of the Taking of Ireland Vol IV* . Dublin:Irish Text Society, 1941

http://www.archive.org/details/leborgablare04macauoft

Proinsias Mac Cana. *Celtic Mythology*, NY: Peter Bedrick Books, 1987

Kim McCone, "Werewolves, Cyclopes, Díberga and Fíanna: Juvenile Delinquency in Early Ireland" *Cambridge Medieval Celtic Studies*, issue 12, 1986

Jim MacDonald's "Jump Kits (Go Bags)" http://www.sff.net/people/doylemacdonald/emerg_kit.htm

Donald MacKinnon, "Fulacht na Morrigna" *The Celtic Review, vol. 8*, 1912

Kuno Meyer, trans. 'The Wooing of Emer'"Tochmarc Emire," *Archaeological Review 1*, 1888,
 http://www.ucc.ie/celt/online/T301021/index.html English, http://www.ucc.ie/celt/published/G301021/index.html Irish

------ *Echtrae Nerai* (The Adventure of Nera) Revue Celtique 10 (1889), pg. 212-228
ucc.ie/academic/smg/CDI/texthtml/echtranerai.html

Joseph Falaky Nagy. *The Wisdom of the Outlaw: The Boyhood Deeds of Finn in Gaelic Narrative Tradition*, Berkeley: University of California Press, 1985

------ *Conversing with Angels and Ancient: Literary Myths of Medieval Ireland.* Ithaca: Cornell University Press, 1997

Muireann Ní Bhrolcháin in "The Banshenshas Revisited," Mary O'Dowd and Sabine Wichert, eds., *Chattle, Servant or Citizen: Women's Status in Church, State and Society*, Belfast: The Institute of Irish Studies, The Queen's University of Belfast, 1995

John O'Donovan, ed. and trans. (with notes and translations from Whitley Stokes) *Sanas Cormaic Calcutta: O. T. Cutter for the Irish Archeological and Celtic Society*, 1868, http://books.google.com/books?id=rX8NAAAAQAAJ&source=gbs_navlinks_s

--------- ed. and trans, Annala Rioghachta Eireann: Annals of the kingdom of *Ireland by the Four Masters, from the earliest period to the year 1616*. Library of the Royal Irish Academy and of Trinity College Dublin Pt 1
http://www.ucc.ie/celt/published/T100005A/index.html English,
http://www.ucc.ie/celt/published/G100005A/index.html Irish

DA Ó Drisceoil, "Burnt Mounds: cooking or bathing?" *Antiquity, 1988, Vol. 62*

Standish Hayes O'Grady, trans., "The Great Defeat on the Plain of Muirthemne before Cuchullin's Death" Eleanor Hull, ed., *The Cuchullin Saga in Irish Literature: being a collection of stories relating to the Hero Cuchullin*, London: David Nutt on the Strand, 1898,
http://www.archive.org/details/cuchullinsagain00cuchgoog

--------, trans. "The Colloquy of the Ancients" Medieval Irish Series, Cambridge, 1999
http://www.yorku.ca/inpar/colloquy_ogrady.pdf

Joseph O'Neill, ed. & trans., "Cath Boinde", *Ériu 2*, 1905, pp. 173-185 http://www.maryjones.us/ctexts/boyne.html

Cecile O'Rahilly, trans., *Táin Bó Cúailnge from Book of Leinster* 1967 ucc.ie/celt/published/T301035/index.html English, ucc.ie/celt/published/G301035/index.html Irish

-------, trans. *Táin Bó Cúailnge, Recession 1* Dublin: Dublin Institute for Advanced Studies, 1976
ucc.ie/celt/published/T301012/index.html English,
ucc.ie/celt/published/G301012/index.html Irish

Nerys Patterson. *Cattle Lords & Clansmen: The Social Structure of Early Ireland*, Notre Dame, IN: University of Notre Dame, 1994

Barry Raftery. *Pagan Celtic Ireland: the Enigma of the Irish Iron Age*, New York: Thames & Hudson, 1994

Royal Irish Academy, *Dictionary of the Irish Language*. Based mainly on Old and Middle Irish Materials at eDil http://www.dil.ie/

The Sarah Connor Charm School Blog fitness articles http://sarahconnorcharmschool.blogspot.com/search/label/fitness

Marie-Louise Sjoestedt, *Celtic Gods and Heroes*, New York: Dover Publications, Inc., Mineola 2000

Tim Smith, "Real Bushcraft And Survival Training Has Nothing To Do With New Age Religion Or Misappropriating Native American Spirituality" on Jack Mountain Bushcraft Blog http://www.jackmtn.com/simplog/?p=133

Maya St.Clair, "An Morrígan: War Goddess and More" on Celtic Scholar's Reviews and Opinions blog http://celticscholar.wordpress.com/2010/05/03/an-morrigan-war-goddess-and-more/

Whitley Stokes, ed., 'Cormac's Glossary' in *Three Irish Glossaries*, London: Williams and Norgate, 1862 http://www.ucd.ie/tlh/text/ws.tig.001.text.html

---------- trans. and ed., "The Second Battle of Moytura" *Revue Celtique* 12 (1891) pg. 52-130, 306-308 archive.org/details/revueceltique12pari

---------- trans, "The Bodleian Dinnshenchas" *Folklore, Vol. 3*, No. 4, Dec., 1892 ucd.ie/tlh/trans/ws.fl.3.001.t.text.html English, ucd.ie/tlh/text/ws.fl.3.001.text.html Irish

---------- trans. and ed., "The Prose Tales in the Rennes Dindshenchas" *Revue Celtique* 15 (1894) pg. 277-236 http://www.archive.org/details/revueceltique15pari

---------- trans. and ed., "The Tragical Death of Cochulainn," Eleanor Hull, ed., *The Cuchullin Saga in Irish Literature: being a collection of stories relating to the Hero Cuchullin*, London: David Nutt on the Strand, 1898, pg. 251-263 http://www.archive.org/details/cuchullinsagain00cuchgoog

-------, ed. *Acallamh na Senórach I*, Stokes & E. Windisch, Irische Texte ser4 1, 1900
ucc.ie/celt/published/G303000/text038.html

Samuel Thayer, *The Forager's Harvest: A Guide to Identifying, Harvesting, and Preparing Edible Wild Plants*, Birchwood, WI: Forager's Harvest Press, 2006

--------- *Nature's Garden: A Guide to Identifying, Harvesting, and Preparing Edible Wild Plants*, Birchwood, WI: Forager's Harvest Press, 2010

Jan Todd, Ph.D. "From Milo to Milo: A History of Barbells, Dumbells, and Indian Clubs" *Iron Game History*, Vol. 3, No. 6, April 1995
http://la84foundation.org/SportsLibrary/IGH/IGH0306/IGH0306c.pdf

AG van Hamel, Compert Con Culainn. And Other Stories Dublin: 1933
archive.org/details/compertconculain03hame

C. Lee Vermeers "Celtic Martial Arts" on A Wolf-Man, Not a Wolf in Man's Clothing Blog
http://faoladh.blogspot.com/2011/04/celtic-martial-arts.html

Máire West, "Aspects of díberg in the tale Togail Bruidne Da Derga" *Zeitschrift für celtische Philologie* (ZcP), *Volume 49-50*, 1997

John "Lofty" Wiseman, *SAS Survival Handbook: For Any Climate, In Any Situation* (revised edition), New York: Collins, 2009

A Wolf-Man, Not a Wolf in Man's Clothing
http://faoladh.blogspot.com/

Jonathan M. Wooding's "Reapproaching the Pagan Celtic Past – Anti-Nativism, Asterisk Reality and the Late-

Antiquity Paradigm" *Studia Celtica Fennica VI*, Finnish Society for Celtic Studies, 2009 pg. 51-74
http://www.sfks.org/Julkaisut.htm

GREAT QUEEN
by Michael Routery

Queen, black
as raven's midnight plumage,
dark feathers brushing lords of battle,
twisting power of the eel
in streaming turbulence,
wolf mother tracking
fury's field --
strength of battle magic,
triple prophetess --
you who helped the
world rise from
chaos at Maige Tuired.

The Blood Crow
by Gerri Leen

Water runs red with the blood
of the soon to be fallen
The Morrigan is about
washing the clothes of the doomed
No kindness in the act
no malice either
Death is her art, her love, her home
War is her domain

Turn a corner, cross a field
See her lover lost
to the fearful bliss
of burying himself in pure desire
The Morrigan flies
with eyes wide open
and sees skies not blue but red
Blood scents her world

Lady Dusk, Mother of Night
by Christa A. Bergerson

sun bleeds
weeps across heavens
she skulks
crawls upon ghost grass
lifts herself
beats her wings
becomes the dusk
swaddles earth in jet
adorned with sparkling stars
and effervescent grandeur

the night
is her warm womb
yearning
to be anointed
longing
to be fed

The Scorned Woman Conjures The Morrigan
by Christa A. Bergerson

Come to me Great Mother Goddess
descend upon them as a cloud
come to me Warrior Queen
envelop them in your shroud

Come to me in the darkened night
swaddle them with your blackened feathers
on the battlefield, amidst all the strife
become their shackle, become their fetters

Come to me Phantom Queen
from out of the amethyst dusk
come to me wondrous Raven
unleash your wild lust

Come to me Wolf of War
I call you from the sorrow of my heart
come to me Bloody Raven
take their heads from their limbs, and tear them apart

How the Morrigan Taught Me to See
by Rebecca Buchanan

open your eyes
to the gruesome
the terrifying
the decaying and the decayed:
there are truths
in such horrors
which others refuse to see:
do not look away

Morrigan in Black and White
by Morgaine Nightshade

You Will Know Me
by Jennifer Lawrence

As strength:
Again and again you raise your weapon,
Fingers gripping tight to the hilt of your saber,
feeling the heaviness of steel as you ready it once more,
feeling the burn in shoulders and back and arms
as you bring it down repeatedly, teeth gritted,
slashing through flesh, hacking through bone,
understanding that the span of your life may be
measured in the number of times you can lift it up again.

As courage:
It takes nerve to bolt up over the top of your fortification,
screaming profanities at the foe as you race toward
the oncoming bullets. Your weapon you tossed aside
before you rose, rushing toward certain death
to scoop up one of your own, one fallen, hurt too badly
to move himself, a friend you refuse to abandon to his certain
      end,
risking your own death just to ensure that, when he passes,
it will be among friends and not face-down in the mud and
      blood.

As fear:
Only the dead and the mad know no terror,
do not feel the quickened rush of breath in their lungs
as they wait for the yellow-green gas to come creeping
through the claustrophobic rabbit-warrens of the trenches.
Those who fear know a single breath will render their insides
to jelly, feeling the hurried thump-thump of their heart as it
frenzies with the hope that the death that makes one
cough out his own insides will not greet him this day.

As rage:
Watching one friend after another get cut down,
dodging each hail of bullets as they speed through the air
like a swarm of angry bees, but whose stingers bring
death instead of just a little pain. You see the shattered faces
of those who met their end at the hands of smiling, laughing
children whose hands reached out not for hugs or sweets,
but to thrust live hand grenades at you, even knowing they
would meet their own end from the handful of green metal.
So many lost for so little, and senseless suffering all around.

As pain:
Under the dull gray-green of the medical tent's roof,
you lay near death, feeling the throbbing agony where
the foot you once had used to be. That phantom sensation
is no less real for all that no foot remains attached to that leg,
nor any flesh whole past the knee. The cannon's ball did its job
all too well, and you draw another tortured breath, listening
as the medics make their way down the line of injured,
listening to the screams as maimed and mangled limbs are
removed, cauterized with a torch, painted with tar. The
doctors are close now, and you lay there with fists clenched,
waiting for your turn with blade and fire, uncertain as to
whether it would be better for the doctors to come before
the last dregs of your life bleed out through shattered bone
and ruined flesh.

As loss:
You can count the numbers of your fallen friends,
but it takes more than the sum of your fingers and toes,
or even those of the few brothers-in-arms that still remain.
You have become well-acquainted with Me, watching as
the carrion-birds strut the field after the battle's end,
feasting richly on the remains of those from both sides,
growing fat as they gorge themselves on eyes and entrails.

You miss those who have gone before you; miss the camaraderie you shared with those you bonded with, knowing that nothing bonds people together more surely than facing death, not knowing which of you will fall and whom will remain behind to mourn those who have already gone on that final journey without you.

As despair:
When you are confronted with the fact that you are fighting and dying for things of no importance, of things that will never change, for causes that have been fought over again and again for centuries, there comes a moment when you realize that you are spending your life, the lives of your fellow soldiers, the lives of the foe, for no reason worth expending the effort -- not even to spit at those who sent you here to die. Then it sinks in, that utter lack of hope, and whether you sit in the dark of night waiting for the blast that will bring it all to an end, or whether you wait under the blazing eye of day, helpless against the forces that have brought you here, you abandon any expectation that you might get out of this hell with flesh and soul and mind unscathed.

As madness:
War is Hell, they say, and amidst the carnage and death there are those who survive even when they wish they had not; broken in body, but more broken in mind, reliving every close call, every explosion, every friend falling dead before their eyes. Those who have gone through this horror and come out the other side carry that Hell inside them always, flinching at every slammed door, every car that backfires, every crash of thunder. Some learn to live with that Hell, embrace it, accept it; others end up giving in to its whispers, taking up arms once again, recreating the battles where they did not die, and felling
      innocents

they imagine as enemies, until they are finally brought down
by those who must oppose them, and are delivered at last
into the shelter of the silent peace they sought --
the peace that only I can bring them.

As numbness:
How many deaths can one see before it ceases to bring grief;
how many stones can be piled upon one's soul before that
soul is crushed underneath the weight of that pain? In the
roar and crash of battle, amid the sweep of rifle fire, only so
much can be registered, can be felt, before even the prospect
of one's own end no longer brings fear, only unfeeling
indifference, and finally longing: an end to strength and
        courage,
fear and rage, loss and madness, pain and despair. All such
        burdens
leave scars, inside and out, and their final sum is the wish for
unending peace: of one sort, or another.

I am War, and Death during War, and all War's horrors.

You will know Me.

Fiction in Her Honor

Bookfront
by Nicole Bonvisuto

Sometimes You Do
by Diotima Sophia

The girls giggled their way into the fortune teller's tent, nervousness vying with bravado for top priority…. The hour was getting late and they'd been on all the rides at the little country fair – most of them twice. They'd hoped, as they always did, to meet "boys" at the fair – but neither of them had much idea of what they would do from there. And of course they had met boys – the local lads from school (who were far too well known to be of interest) and the young men who travelled with the fair (who were far too grown up to be safe – their presence was one reason the girls always came to the fair together).

So now, as most people were thinking of going home, the girls decided to give the fortune teller a try. Genny's grandmother and Ali's mother would be scandalized when they found out, which was a good enough reason to chance it, they felt. Neither girl really expected to hear anything startling … but they could hope.

The interior of the booth was dark, made darker still when the lights from the nearer rides began to go out. Clutching each other's hands, the girls look round, at the sparkly shawl draped across the mirror, at the rickety little table with an empty chair on either side of it..

"And me. Be welcome, if you so would be."

The old woman seemed to have appeared out of nowhere, but Genny at least noticed that her hand was still holding the edge of a black curtain – when it dropped into place behind the old woman, there was no way to tell it was not actually one side of the booth's main walls. Genny marked this to the plus side of the register in her mind – it was a neat trick to have even a tiny room hidden in a tent this small.

The old woman seated herself behind the table and waved an open hand at the empty chair.

"Who will ask me first, their fortune?"

Each of the girls tried to push the other forward – in the end, Ali sat down at the table.

"Shall I cross your palm with silver?" she asked in a breathless attempt at humour. It would have worked – if it hadn't been clear that she was half serious.

"No – gold will do – or the colour thereof. 'A pound in the plate and your fortune told.'" The old woman repeated it like a mantra.

Giggling still, Ali dropped a coin on the flat plate in front of her and looked up expectantly. The old woman held out a hand – at first Ali thought she was asking for more money, but then realised it was her palm that was required.

The old woman bent over Ali's hand for a moment, and then looked up at her, "You will marry before you're 20, bear before 25, and bring up strong sons for your family."

Ali stared at her – she'd expected the "tall, handsome stranger" line. "Who? Who will I marry?"

"Such details are not clear, my dear. Be assured, he will not be local."

That pleased Ali inordinately – any boy from the next big city was considered a foreigner and therefore exotic, in the village. Then a thought occurred to her.

"Sons? Won't I have any girls?"

The old woman didn't speak – merely sat with her arms crossed, looking silently at the girl before her, as though .... She were expecting something?

Ali was forming her question again (maybe the old woman hadn't understood?), when her phone went off, bringing a discordantly modern note into the dark little booth.

"'Scuse me," Ali said, and held the phone to her ear, looking more and more concerned with every passing second. She finally said, "I'll be there." Ignoring the old woman now completely, Ali turned to Genny and said, "I'm going to take the taxi to the hospital – mum's collapsed again. Johnny's already there."

"I'll go with you!" Genny knew as well as Ali did what another collapse meant, and though Ali and her brother were close, she wanted to be there, too.

"No, I'll go alone. I want to – I … need to. Johnny's there".

Genny started to protest, but the old woman cut across her. "Sometimes, you have to do what needs to be done." She covered Ali's hand with her own, and said, "Go now – it will be well." The words seemed to echo in the little tent. Then Ali had run out, leaving Genny standing there.

"Come, will you not have your fortune told, too?"

"You didn't predict that!" Genny pointed to the door her friend had just used.

"Well, I didn't mention it, put it that way." The old woman's speech was suddenly much more normal than it had been. "I told her what she wanted to know, and it was hardly difficult to predict, after all. She's young, strong and pretty – so it's all terribly, drearily predictable."

"And me?" Genny was standing behind the chair -- she felt no inclination to sit in it, though.

"You're … different." The old woman shrugged. "Oh, you're young and strong, yes – which is just as well. You're not as pretty as your friend" (Genny winced, even though she knew it was true), "but in the end you're far more attractive. And much less predictable." She smiled.

"Do you want to see my hand?"

"Do you think I need it?"

It was a question, not a challenge – the old woman genuinely interested in the answer.

"I don't know," Genny said, slowly. "But … if I were guessing, I'd guess not – I'm not sure there's much you do need, to be honest."

The old woman nodded, "Good – awareness of what you know, and willingness to chance what you don't. It bodes well."

"Pardon?" Genny didn't know whether to be worried about Ali or not – in fact, she was beginning to wonder if she should be worried for herself.

"D'you doubt me, girl?"

"Yes, frankly. I don't understand you. You keep changing." And indeed, it wasn't just the old woman's language that was changing – she seemed different, somehow. And more lights were going off in the fairground, so the little booth was getting even darker.

"Indeed I do. Change, that is. Change is … all." She held Genny's gaze, steadily. Genny found herself standing taller, and gripping the back of the chair in front of her, for support.

"Will you be ready – for change?" The woman – who no longer seemed nearly so old – rose, and placed both hands on the table, leaning across it toward Genny.

"Change – great change. That's your future – be prepared for it. Change – ride it like a wave, don't fight it like an enemy. Embrace it like a lover and it will bear fruit; run from it, and it will destroy you."

In the changing light from the last ride left, her eyes glazed red, and the now young woman said, "Change. It is your lot. Be it so."

Dropping the chair – which she hadn't remembered lifting, but realised she had been holding like a shield – Genny turned and ran from the booth ….

In the tiny back room of "Gypsy Tamar's Fortune Telling Booth," Audrey came out of a deep sleep, peopled with strange dreams. (She'd been given that entirely mundane name in the hope that she would not take after her rather eccentric grandmother, whom she so resembled. It had been a forlorn hope. In the perverse way these things worked, she'd become all that her granny had been, and more. Being a fairground fortune teller was a wonderful job, she'd found – no matter what strange things happened around her, people always assumed it was "done with mirrors"). Realising she'd slept the entire evening, she raised the curtain to the main booth – and was surprised to see a pound coin gleaming in the plate. Through the gloom, she could just make out another shape ... resting? ... perched? ... on the chair. A bird? Ah, a raven?

Even though they'd pitched in the country this time, there was no natural explanation for a raven perching in her booth at midnight – so she assumed that the answer wasn't entirely "natural" and a not very great leap of the imagination to her to the right answer.

That didn't mean she particularly wanted to share the booth for the rest of the night, however, so she held open the outer door of tent and said, "Lady, if you will?"

As the bird hopped from one foot to another – apparently enjoying the feel of antique oak in its claws, Audrey stood patiently by the open door. She couldn't help but wonder, though… why here? Why now?

As the bird flew out past her, with the dying light of the very last ride reflecting on its ebony plumage, she seemed to hear, from far away, "Sometimes, you have to do what needs to be done."

Shell Shock
by Juli D. Revezzo

Antonia barely grunted as she threw her student to the mat. She winced when she heard the boards beneath him crunch. She'd let the fight run away with her again. *Damn.* Students lined up around the block to learn her techniques, for this sole reason. Sometimes, she forgot where she was. Humans were far too fragile.

This is not a battlefield, Antonia.

She leaned down and offered him her hand. "Are you all right, Tyler?"

He groaned as he sat up but was too manly to let her see she'd hurt him. She knew it, though, could read it in his slow movements; saw it in the red-black flare of his aura. She laid a hand on his shoulder. "Good work, Tyler. Thanks for demonstrating. You'll have that black belt yet."

Tyler hobbled away. Antonia reminded her class that she would be overseas next week -- and for an undetermined amount of time -- on family business. Her feet barely whispered across the dojo's wooden floors as she walked to the locker rooms. She twirled her staff in her right hand, nonchalantly, gaze skimming over the awards, photographs, and tiger-decorated banners gracing the walls. Catching the staff in her left hand, she unscrewed it, at its midsection, and flipped the two pieces through the air as she came into the ladies' dressing room. Approaching her locker, she opened its door, and pulled a black and gray gym bag out. Setting it down to unzip it, she tucked the staff inside, and pulled forth a towel.

Having showered, and been restored to a semblance of civility, she slid into her army green slacks, and tight gray camouflage tee shirt.

"Subtle, Toni." Lucille's soft voice sounded from the other side of the dressing room.

Antonia turned to the source, and smiled, but she didn't like the look on her face. "Lu, what's wrong?"

"Can we go somewhere quiet?" Lucille paused, brown eyes blank, for a moment. "For lunch? I need to talk to you. My treat."

Antonia blinked and dropped her long red hair, forgetting the ponytail on which she'd been so intent. "Sure. Of course. I know just the place; follow me there. I don't want to worry about your car, while we're away."

* * *

Antonia didn't like it. The look on Lucille's expression was far too serious. The news was even worse.

Her sister had slit her wrists once.

"Just to see what it was like," Lucille now insisted.

Antonia narrowed her eyes, the sounds of the café fading into the background as she processed the information. Lucille had really done it. She couldn't believe her sister was so stupid. It was probably just as well that she waited twenty years to reveal this secret. Had she known about it sooner, she would've killed Lucille herself. Now, she could only glower. "Lucille, you have better things to do than that. Don't be so damned stupid. And don't tell *her* about it!" Antonia said. "The Morrigan needs us. I don't think she would appreciate such a confession -- especially now. The desert is no place for it."

"I'm not telling her," Lucille insisted. "I'm telling *you*."

"Yes, well -- " Antonia got to her feet. "Keep it between us."

They had a long way to go -- but not really very far at all. Lucille, to her credit, remained silent about the whole suicide experiment. If she mentioned it again, Antonia was so furious, she might haul off and give her a black eye. The Morrigan would definitely not approve of that.

Antonia was grateful when her sister changed the subject. As they boarded their plane and settled into their seats, Lucille chatted about mundane things. Husbands (of which she had had too many), children (likewise, too many), the books and authors that obsessed her these days, all the reasons why people were deluded about the world around them formed the bulk of their conversation, not the coming battle. Lucille and she may be sisters, but sometimes, Antonia wondered if perhaps her family had adopted Lucille. Her nervousness, her avoidance of a subject she loved above all others, made Antonia suspicious of her sister's roots. Lucille acted more like a frightened child, sometimes, than the woman she should be.

"You're no better!" Lucille snapped.

"At least I don't marry mine."

"That's my point," Lucille insisted. "Do you know what that makes you? You have way too many notches on your bedpost, my dear."

Antonia ignored her, and asked the stewardess for a cup of coffee. She hadn't slept in a week ... too long. She'd spent last night with a general; the night before that ... a veteran from the battlefields in Afghanistan -- she'd had several of them lately. She even fancied a certain married politician -- or he fancied her, as the case was.

"Occupational hazard," Antonia answered. The stewardess returned and Antonia took and tasted her coffee, wasting time flipping the spoon in her hand as she waited for the stewardess to retreat out of earshot. "You can't take it, Lu. I can." Stabbing the spoon at the tray before her, she added, "If you'd like to share that job, I'd welcome you. I could use more sleep."

"No." Lucille frowned. "No thanks. I don't like your sleep patterns. When you sleep -- "

Listening to her sister continue her one-sided conversation, Antonia worried. Something was really bothering Lucille. Had she spoken of this to anyone else? Where had she been, recently? She suddenly realized she should have spent last night with a very different Veteran.

Antonia politely interrupted her sister, and excused herself. She strolled the plane's aisle, knowing who she was looking for, and seeking him out, all the same. There, four rows down and on the left side of the plane, she spotted a soldier typing on his laptop. She approached him, cleared her throat, and smiled sweetly down upon him as she spoke. "I'm sorry to bother you. Might I trouble you for a few minutes of your access, there?" She waved a hand to the computer. "I need to email something to my superiors -- urgently -- and -- " She whipped the spoon in the air, but he saw something very different in her hand: A cell phone. "My battery died."

"Certainly, Ma'am." His southern accent was thick, as was his gentlemanly air, despite the alpha bravado she knew he favored in other company. He clicked a few keys, while Antonia squatted next to him, waiting patiently. Finished, the soldier turned the computer around in his lap.

She smiled brightly, taking in the fact that he wore no wedding ring, and turned her eyes to the screen. Deftly she accessed the Internet, and her email account.

To: Col. Ted McMasterson
From: Antonia McBainon.
En route now.
ETA 600 hours.
PS. Lu Kimbeon distressed. I suspect mild shell shock.
Please advise.

Antonia signed off with her usual farewell, went back to the soldier's main screen, and politely thanked him as she handed the computer back. She stood, turned, but then on second thought, turned back to the soldier. "Thank you," she said for the second time. "I mean, for your service. We don't tell our soldiers that, often enough. I think we should get more thanks for what we do, don't you?"

"Yes, ma'am," he agreed. "You're in the military?" He studied her thoughtfully for a moment. "I wouldn't've guessed."

Antonia raised a mischievous red eyebrow. "There's much you wouldn't believe about me, Corporal." The soldier blinked blue eyes. Did he see what she was? Did he understand what kind of soldier she was -- what she'd done in battle -- when she said such a thing? "It's not something I can talk about. Top secret, you understand." He nodded thoughtfully, and in return, thanked her for what she likely did, day in, day out.

That was all she needed. Antonia leaned down again, close to the young man's ear. "I'm in the back," she purred. "There's an empty seat next to me, if you'd like it."

The soldier's denim-blue eyes went wide, studying her now in a combination of intrigue and shock. Antonia smiled, stood, and walked back to her seat, certain he followed. She knew Lucille would tease her for this.

* * *

By the time they arrived, Lucille was furious with her; Antonia didn't care. Her new friend, the 3rd Division Infantryman, was happy and back in his own seat, head down, studying something on his computer. Nonetheless, he'd already found an excuse to stretch his legs once, in her direction.

Antonia winked at him as she passed by on the way to disembark to the Paris airport terminal. She wanted to keep that young man in sight, of that she was sure. Right now, she had a very different set of young men in mind. She was glad that at least her corporal, there, would sit out battle, for the time being.

Paris was far better than where he'd been, and far better than where she'd be, tomorrow morning. She glanced over at her sister.

"You all right, Lu?" No one would have to press her into admitting her sister looked far from fine. She looked ragged, distant in Antonia's opinion, her eyes almost blank as she took in the evening traffic. "Would you like to stay here? The Morrigan will understand."

She wasn't so sure about that, but it was worth it if the thought might help Lucille. She did look more than a little frazzled.

"No," Lucille slung her bag over her shoulder and jammed her hands in her pockets. "No, I don't think she would. I'm fine, Toni; don't worry about me."

Antonia laid a hand on her shoulder. "You can wait here. It will be fine."

But Lucille was insistent. She would travel on.

Antonia sighed. "Let's get some coffee. Irish coffee, if you like."

Lucille rewarded her with a smile, half-hearted though it seemed. "Just the thing for a night like this."

"Agreed." Antonia laughed, but it died as her sister turned her back on her. *It was going to be a long one.*

She hoped Lucille would finally see reason and stay behind. Summer, in Paris, after all ... The city held an intrigue even Lucille couldn't ignore. Antonia knew she couldn't. But there was work ahead, elsewhere.

* * *

"Desert brown," Lucille complained, squinting into the morning sun, "is definitely not my color."

Antonia sighed and refrained from arguing that she had adored it, only last year. "I know, sis. Come." She trudged ahead, kicking sand as she went. There, ahead of them, their troops: Hum Vees, tanks, tents, men and women dressed, like her in desert khaki fatigues. These were not the soldiers on whom Antonia was intent.

Before the American, British, and Allied troops, on a ridge to the west, stood a horde the likes of which those troops would only now see in films. She hoped. Could the British, the Americans, the Allies see them? Did they know they were among the lines of their squadrons? Did they understand the true size of their army?

Probably not. They saw Hum Vees, tanks, tents; the drab adobe buildings of the town below, the dust blowing around them, obscuring everything in a thin haze. On the edge of the battleground, the American and British allies cleaned modern-day guns, eyeing the area with worried suspicion. Yet the soldiers were completely oblivious to the hordes of warhorses and strong, armored men and women in their midst, the ancient weaponry hidden behind cloaks of time-steeled illusion.

It was to these horsemen and women that Antonia trudged, all of them intent on every movement made by yet another woman, one with long black hair, pulled back in a ponytail.

She was beautiful. Antonia almost couldn't look at her, and so turned her attention to the horses, and their riders; Lucille was tending to hers, and joking with another soldier. The horse snorted in a tinny breath. Before Antonia could speak, she heard the General's voice. "Lucille, Antonia, come here, please."

She turned, smiled to see the General's gaze locked on hers.

"Antonia? Lucille?"

Antonia's gaze returned to the sunlit city before them. Lucille caught up with her. "What's up?"

"I don't know."

As they reached her side, the General pointed to the knot of soldiers nearby. "Lucille, check over this battalion, for me. I'll be right back."

Lucille studied her a moment, her eyes shifting colors and countenance as she did so. Antonia smiled to see the change: her pupils shifting from the singular form of the world of men, to the three of the people to whom she owed her birthright.

Perhaps she would not regret her decision to return to the battle.

"I'm fine," Lucille assured her. "You'll see."

Antonia laid a hand on her shoulder. "No worries, Lu. I'll let you know if there's any important word for you, all right?"

Lucille looked over her shoulder to the men of their regiment, then back to the ridge and the raven-haired General. "Our sister will not be happy I'm ignoring her, but .... All right." She scratched fingers through her red hair, mussing it a bit. "Keep me posted."

Antonia nodded, and walked away to join the black-haired general. "Morrigan--sister." She paused, bent a knee in obeisance, as she approached. "I apologize for our delay. It was—"

"She came. I didn't think she would." The Morrigan cocked a dark brow. "Is she well?"

Antonia glanced over her shoulder, then back to the awesome woman before her and winced under her piercing gaze. The Morrigan's power, her very presence, coated the world in the aura of doom so thick, sometimes without willing it to. That power made Antonia hyperventilate.

She stepped aside, not taking her eyes from the Morrigan, in order to let a truck full of British soldiers, and their assorted weaponry, pull up to the ridge beside her and the raven-haired General. "I don't know, my lady. Honestly? I don't think she should've come."

The Morrigan slanted a glance in Lucille's direction. "Do you truly think she's suffering shell shock?" The look on the Morrigan's face was utter astonishment. "How is that possible for one of my children?"

Antonia shook her head. "I don't know. I only know she's not at her best, right now. I fear it was a mistake for her to leave ... home."

The Morrigan gave a weary, annoyed grunt. Then she turned and left her position overlooking the town, walking with steps almost light and airy as she moved among the ranks of her eager, mounted horsemen. Each saluted, and she duly acknowledged their respect. Coming to Lucille's side, where she checked her tack, the Morrigan cleared her throat. The soldiers snapped to attention. "Lucille," she said. "I've heard of your troubles. You need not join us in this operation."

Lucille's eyes went wide. "My sister? I don't know what you mean."

The Morrigan shifted her triple-pupiled eyes to the men around Lucille, all of whom were now curiously attentive to their General's conversation. She looked back to Lucille. "Your regiment will sit this battle out. Take your rest. We will see to this." She paused a moment, and then added, "That's an order."

Lucille gulped. "Yes, my Lady."

The Morrigan stepped away to inspect the horses and Antonia took her place by Lucille's side. "You should've stayed in Paris when you had the chance."

Lucille watched her men turn their horses from the field. "Maybe I'll catch the next plane back."

Antonia laid a hand on her shoulder, smiled. "That's what I'd do. If you see a certain corporal on the way -- "

"I know. He's yours."

Antonia laughed, and Lucille kissed her cheek and followed her men to safety. Antonia frowned after them, fanned herself to drive away the desert heat as she walked to her assembled regiment. It was shaping up to be a blistering day. Content with her men and their state of readiness, Antonia turned back to the ridge. Threading her way through the American and British soldiers now assembling, itching for battle, as she was herself, even as the sky lightened, ticking down the minutes until dawn, she came upon the Morrigan.

She stood beside a Hum Vee, leaning against its door, watching her. "We're ready, my sister."

The Morrigan nodded gravely. "You're sure? You don't share Lucille's ... worries, do you?"

Antonia paused in her tracks, aghast at the notion. "No, my lady; thankfully, no."

"I've always suspected -- " She sighed, not finishing her statement.

Antonia narrowed her eyes at her sister. "What?"

The Morrigan smiled. "You are made of stronger stuff than she. It's why you're good at what you do, why I trust you to do your job." She flicked her strange eyes to the soldiers inside the vehicle.

Antonia peered through the open window, watching two handsome young men. She read the driver's name, smiled sweetly as he clearly took notice of her, and greeted her, in a thick British accent. "I think," she said, "this will go well, don't you? Tell you what, Private McManus, I'll watch your back for you; I trust you'll watch mine?"

The soldier blinked green eyes, and smiled. "I'd like that." His voice gave away a hint of Scottish beneath the British ring. "If we don't get separated in the melee."

"*If.*" Antonia knew what he feared -- and that he had a right to fear it. She nodded to something inside the vehicle: a stack of CD cases. "What's in your collection? I prefer the old Metal, myself. Do you have any of that?"

"I think not," the Morrigan cut in. "The Corporal and I share similar tastes. I think he knows what I mean." She raised a dark eyebrow. "Don't you think it's in order today?"

The man nodded, nudged his friend and pointed to the CDs. "You know the one?" His friend smiled and pulled a CD from the stack. Antonia's nose twitched as she read the name. She loved them, too, but wasn't in the mood to ruin that love, for these young men. "My lady, please." The goddess might blast her for such a direct disagreement. Antonia steeled herself for the strike.

It didn't come.

"Not that one," she pleaded.

"You don't like it?" McManus's friend asked, sliding the CD home, and turning the volume knob. "Come on, you can't hate this. It's -- "

" -- too cool," the driver agreed, winking at her. "You have to love this one. I do."

"No, I agree. It is more than appropriate." She bobbed her head slightly to the opening strains of the now unbearably loud song on which the Morrigan doted. Oh, well. Let him remember that fondly. It would be his last hearing of the song here in this world. She wished the young men well, and turned away to return to her own troops. The Morrigan smiled at the young men and walked away and Antonia thought she might try to bargain a nice place for this McManus, in the Otherworld, if she had to give away an eye in the mix.

She took one last liberty, and turned to the Morrigan to voice her protest. The Morrigan simply smiled, shrugged. "He shall have wherever you wish," she said. "Join your men."

Antonia nodded in acceptance, and turned away from the truck and the General, smiling to hear the Morrigan's voice softly singing the battle cry of the song's opening lines. As she ran to join her men, overhead, she saw shadowy Valkyries on horseback wheeling through the sky. *The gang's all here.*

Almost.

She mounted her steel-veiled red stallion, and focused intently on the Morrigan, standing before them, on the ridge ahead. Antonia worried for her missing sister. She worried for the soldier she'd taken a liking to, just now, and hoped she was wrong. She hoped the Morrigan wouldn't forget her promise. She hoped shell shock was the worst of their troubles. She hoped her shell-shocked sister returned soon. She hoped to return home empty-handed tonight.

She hoped not to.

The Hum Vees, Jeeps, tanks, and trucks began to rev their engines. Antonia's horse, and those of her troops, stamped the ground impatiently. There was a signal they awaited; she knew it, her troops knew it, even if the British, the Americans, and their Allies around them did not. She smiled as it came ...

The Morrigan, standing before them, raised an M1 machine gun high into the air.

Antonia gripped her AK-47. Watching the American and British soldiers and their modern weaponry begin to roll, she gave a wild battle cry. She spurred her stallion into a breakneck run, and joined the chaotic battle with the insurgents below.

Macha's Curse
by Stephanie Woodfield

The Morrigan is a frequent visitor in my dreams. At times she is the battle raven, imparting wisdom on black wings. Other times she is a woman with dark hair, a spear or sword in hand, challenging me to live up to my full potential. Experiencing deity in that mist-filled world between waking consciousness and the worlds that lay beyond can be profound. It is rare though that I ever dream of being a deity. I may encounter the gods, call upon them, but only once have I even had an encounter with deity in my dreams where I acted as that deity and experienced that god's acts and thoughts as if they were my own. It is an experience that left me scrabbling for a pen upon waking and filled me with a unique sense of communion. So here is Macha's story, from her eyes, from that watery realm of dreams where we all can walk (or run) a mile in a goddess's shoes.

***

The dappled mare beside me stomps the ground impatiently just as the child within my womb begins to kick. She eyes me wearily, perhaps knowing better than the men who gather around us what I am. Another kick from the life within me; the mare dances nervously in place kicking up clumps of packed earth with her hooves, and I run a hand over my swollen stomach. Although I know it is pointless, I call out to the crowd again. It is too close to my time, will they not wait till after I have brought this tiny life into the world to test my husband's foolish bragging? But my plea is met with laughter. I look at the bearded faces around me; did a mother not bare each of them? How can they listen with such deaf ears and stony hearts to my pleas? I place a protective hand on my belly again, and think that if this had been a crowd of women I would not be answered with jeers. Little do they know this was never about the race; the race is already won.

My pleas unanswered, the signal is given and the horses run free. I begin slowly, following behind them on the track. Their hooves pound against the earth, like distant thunder, like the beat of the drums within the Sidhe hills. I concentrate on the sound, and as I run I change. What the men see I do not know. Do they see the pale woman with hair the color of flame? Or do they see the roan mare? Perhaps both? When I run I am free, the weight of the world disappears as if a great yoke has been cast off my shoulders. There is nothing I cannot outrun. I am as eager as that dappled mare to challenge the wind, and so I run, and run, and run. The crowd blurs around me, a few shout in disbelief as I easily pass the king's chariot. This was not what they expected. They were so certain these beasts where the swiftest that ever lived. Perhaps they are, but at this moment I am the Great Mare, I am the primal essence of every horse that ever was, and there is nothing that I cannot outrun, nothing I cannot overcome. But this magick has a price, and I will have to pay it all too soon.

When I cross the finish line I collapse, no longer the Great Mare, but a woman in the final stages of labor. The crowd circles around me. These men of sword and spear, who spill blood and glory in death, I wonder, do they know the value of life? They are so close, life and death, both forged in blood and pain, whether it be the pangs of labor or the sting of a blade. Transitions are never easy, whether we are coming into this world or leaving it behind. They look at me in astonishment, unsure of what to do or say. They should have waited as I had asked. Did I not deserve that much mercy? Do they think my husband's boast was so bold now? I think not, but it was never about the boast, or the race. I knew from the very moment they arrived at my doorstep that I would win. It was about the mercy of men. It was about honoring the women who bore them, and the women who will bare their own children, and their children's children.

I feel myself fading as I hear my child cry out. No, as my children cry out. Twins. Despite the pain, I smile. Someone places them in my arms, a tiny mercy, although it is too little, too late. I look into my children's faces and both a fierce love and a fierce rage spark within my broken body. I feel the blood pouring from me. It comes too quickly. The womb that brought life into the world will soon end mine, but there is still some magick left in me, and when I speak it is not as a dying woman, but as a Goddess.

Some will call it a curse. But in my mind it is a blessing. For nine generations, in the hour of their greatest need, the bearded men of Ulster will know the pangs of a woman in childbed. If men will take life and throw it away so carelessly on idle words they will know the pain, the sacrifice, it took to bring life into the world. Perhaps then they will not throw it away so carelessly.

With the last word of my spell my human body gives way. Once more I am myself, shining spirit, immortal fay, Goddess. My sisters never understood my desire to take on mortal flesh for a time. They both warned it would only cause me pain. And it has, but it has also brought two new lives into the world. Two flames that will shine brightly, if only for a little while.

The crowd stands in stunned silence around my discarded mortal frame. As I watch, my spirit begins to take on a familiar shape: sleek wings, and black glossy feathers like a cloak of midnight. No one sees the crow now perched on one of the raceway's posts. As I fly away I wonder if they will see my curse for what it truly is.

Through the Gloom
by Diotima Sophia

There were vultures up there somewhere, he supposed. But they were lost in the growing gloom – sunset already? Well, his sunset anyway – he knew well enough that he'd never see another dawn. The gloom might be only his – or his and that of those around him still able to see anything at all.

No vultures yet, then – but the crows. Tens of them – hundreds – thousands? He decided not to waste his remaining minutes counting them – he'd rather curse them, and all they represented. Harbingers of death, indeed – and of ....

Even now, at this nearly-end point, he couldn't bring himself to think Her name. His tribe revered her, as any good warfaring group was sensible to do, but there was a healthy dose of fear mixed into the reverence.

Though, when he thought about it, there was no harm in calling Her now – if today's activities hadn't attracted Her, then the mere enunciation of a short name would hardly do so.

Minutes ... hours? later, he realised that he'd drifted off, and came back to himself with a start. Almost clinically, he ran his mind around his body, noting the discomfort of the rutted turf under his back, the graze on his sword arm – even the blister left by the ill fitting boot. Anything to distract himself from the gaping, sucking wound in his gut that he knew would take his life before long.

Another period of unconsciousness was, he felt, rudely interrupted by scrabbling sounds close to him. He realised that there would be those who came to divest the fallen of treasure (some hope! If they'd had treasure, they'd have stayed home, safe and warm!), weapons, (those, at least, had served him well today – he could, with an effort, still feel the sword under his hand), even boots (and he heartily wished whomever inherited his would suffer with the same blisters). He also knew the other work of such scavengers, and didn't know if he would welcome or fear the "kindly blade" when it came.

The noise grew nearer. He summoned his waning strength -- a warrior should face death with his eyes open. (He felt a moment of satisfaction that the thrust that was draining his life away – slowly, so slowly! – was in his front – there were no scars on his back). Well, none from the warfare of men -- and another, far more pleasant interlude occurred as he recalled gaining the scratches that were there.

"Caw!"

The insistent, impertinent cry of the crow recalled him – he hated it more than ever now. He'd been hoping to die while reveling in the memory of Alwyn. Her swollen belly had only caused them to be more creative – it certainly hadn't slowed them down. But now, he was here. Again. Rooted to the battlefield.

Literally.

For the first time he acknowledged the sword that kept him pinned to the earth.

He supposed he would have died much sooner if it'd been removed – but the man who wielded it had fallen as soon as the deed was done. So the sword remained, an obscene marker in the land of the dead and dying.

Perhaps that's what had attracted the crow, which regarded him with its head cocked to one side.

He found, to his anger, that he had neither voice to shout at it nor strength to raise his hand to it. He had to be content to glare at it – and his glare had controlled his tribe for years – perhaps it would avail with a bird?

Seemingly ... not.

The bird hopped closer – intrigued to see eyes moving as it was used to the eyes of men on battlefields being already fixed.

And then, he heard it, above the cawing of the crows, the groans of the dying, even above the distant sounds of the victors' celebrations – a cry.

A woman's cry.

Alwyn's cry – of pain, and triumph.

And he knew, even here, a day's ride away – that his son was born. He was amazed to find that almost dead as he was, the tears still came.

Through the mist of tears, the mists of death, he looked back to the crow. But instead – She was there, cradling a child. His child.

"She is safe. A birth – a death. It was ever so. For such is life – and such am I."

In wonder, in awe, his body succumbed as it should have done hours earlier.

The Lady smiled. And, as a courtesy to her faithful warrior, closed his eyes before the crows descended.

Morrigan, Wolf-Eyed
by Sarah Sinopa

The Morrigan's Story
by Rufus Brock Maychild

Between the Worlds, between Life and Death, there is a River. You may well find Me there, at the Ford. Let me tell you of one who came by ....

I was kneeling by the waters, washing a shroud. That's usually how people see Me anyway. What I really do is to wash from the spirit-bodies of those who come enough of the Pain of Life that they can Cross the River, and not stay, mortal-side, stuck in their pain. I untie the knot that binds them to mortality.

He came striding up the mountain (most people find the ford as if it's in a mountain pass), brisk as you could wish with his old-fashioned boots and rucksack. He looked happy enough – he remembered the hills he had walked before – and he well remembered too that for the last few years of life he had been so crippled with arthritis that he could barely get out of a chair in time not to wet himself. He wasn't too sure where he was right now, but he knew well enough where he wanted to get to. Jack, his name was.

So often people fear Me. Such silly stories. Some have called me a Goddess of War (as if such a thing were possible!). Of course, sometimes those close to death have seen me on a battlefield, or one of my strong Daughters -- seen Our hands reaching into the hearts of the screaming, giving them surcease, helping the dying get free and be on their way. It takes such blood and pain to give birth to a child, and so many years to raise, yet so few seconds to destroy. How could any Goddess revel in that? Call My Name as they will, I give nothing to those who slaughter in their greed and lust for power. They also will come to me.

Well, to get back to my tale -- Jack didn't bat an eyelid when he saw me there. He gave me a look (I seemed to him as an old woman, of course) and said[11], to my considerable surprise:

"Ee pet, tha hands will be fair clemmed in that water. Let me rinse that for thee."

And he just knelt down, took the shroud from me and got to the washing! It didn't take him very long, and after a while, he tossed it to the far side of the little stream that the River appeared to be. (It's not the same for everyone -- for those few that come here living, the River is wide, deep and thick, red as blood, and even fewer of them return this way.)

He gave me another look, and then, to my even greater surprise, said:

"Wouldst tha like me to brush thy hair pet -- I ken it's hard when tha hands get stiff."

No one had ever asked that before! I don't remember having a hairbrush, but he picked one up and set to work. My hair is almost as long as time itself, and it had a knot for every soul that had died unloved. It was clear he was practised at this task. He was very patient and gentle. So it took him a long long time, but that was nothing to me. I hold time in my hands. As he brushed, my hair changed from silver to black.

But all things come to their end. If I were a pussycat I would have been purring! He put down the brush and looked at me for a third time. I knew that now he could see the stars about Me. He bowed his head and said:

"I'm sorry, Ma'am ... if I've been familiar ... I thought thou was my Mary. I'm on my way to her, I think."

"No, not your Mary," I said. "I am She Who Waits. All come to Me, though few have met Me with such kindness in

---

[11] *Jack speaks with an accent characteristic of North-East England, popularly 'Geordie'*

their hands. And your Mary's not so far now – across the stream and just a little further, you'll meet her again."

He was about to make a quickly respectful departure when something caught his eye. On the far side of the ford, the shroud he'd washed had swollen up, and something was now bursting from it. Much like a butterfly from its cocoon, but this was certainly human. Quite a nice-looking young chap too -- rather like Jack ...

But Jack just splashed straight across the stream in his great old boots without another look at me, and was hugging the boy and laughing. He had last seen this face long years before, deep under the earth. His own hands had ripped as he tried to pull the rocks off the broken body of his son.

Then off the two of them stomped, without so much as a glance back. They will soon have found their Mary. Such fierce pride they all had. Such fearless lust for life they had. I suspect they won't rest for long before they make make the leap back.

Not many do stay to talk with Me. I remember Boudicca, the Great Queen, of course. She had called on Me, that her hand might not through fear falter in its choice. That dreadful night, she sat with Me as every one of the long, long line passed us by. Unnumbered our tears, the River in flood below us. At last, she too passed on, in silence. I am the grave of every mortal hope.

I ask of you, that when you too come to Me, you will stop a while and share your story. Drink with Me, from My Cup, that is the Lake of Memory, before moving on, and in lives to come you will never thirst. I am Boundless, All Being Is In My Mantle. I promise that I will be here to greet you.

New Word
by Diotima Sophia

"And now, go!" Holding out an imperious arm, she faded from their view ... leaving them awestruck.

Why they should be so, she mused, was a different matter. After all, they'd gone to all that trouble to call her ....

"Yeah, but that's just it, innit?"

"What?" Flexing her shoulders dislodged him. He appeared to be in one of his rare talkative moods, however.

"Well, they goes through all that stuff – chanting, candles, and all that malarkey – cause that's what's important to them, y'see."

"What's important to them, dear bird," she said gently "is me."

"Y'see, that's where you're wrong there," he said from the (he hoped) safe distance away where he'd landed. He was certainly out of arm's reach – whether he was out of harm's reach, he wasn't sure. However, he still seemed to be in one piece, so ... "infera penny, infera poun'" as his granny had been wont to say. "Look, it's not that they don't want to see you – it's just that they never expects to – don't ya see? I mean, you don't go every time, do ya?"

"Every time someone calls me? Of course not. I have things to do other than that." She settled her robe around her a bit more, intrigued and amused at the conversation.

"And they've got used to that, y'see? The calling is more important than the answer to 'em, anymore. Then you goes and shows up and puts the wind right up 'em, you do."

And looking at her smug expression, he realised he'd never been in any danger at all because he wasn't telling her anything new at all. And she knew the effect she was having. The smug smile said it all.

"Yeah, ok, fair dos, you knew it already. So, why d'ya do it at all? Why not just let 'em get on with it?"

"And how long, do you think, would they keep on with it, if I never answered?" She nodded to him, and continued. "Just enough – that's the answer. Too much – it'd be common place, everyday, boring. Too little – they'd forget, give up. Just enough ... just enough ...."

"Yeah, but you used to do it a lot more. Wha' happened?"

"They changed. They lost the wonder they used to have. Now, if something is easy, if something is common, it has no value to them. They are incapable, any more, of awe at the real – they bow only to the fantastic, the unusual. The numinous, they miss, overlook."

"Numer ... numon ... the what?" He hopped from one foot to the other in confusion.

She held out a hand and he came back to her. "Numinous, black bird. Think of a shining mist. Numinous, the presence of deity. Think: how do you know I'm here?"

He cocked his head at her and gently prodded her with his beak. "I knows you're there cause I see you. How hard is that?"

"Not hard at all. But then, you see what's there."

"Oh, I gets it. They don't?"

"Not anymore. Too far away from what's real. Too many layers between their hearts and minds."

"Ok, I'm with you now. So, you only show up ...?"

"When those layers are susceptible to breaking, bird."

"And then they see you." It was a statement.

"More. They see and remember."

He nodded, which, to his annoyance, came out as an avian bobbing movement, not a nod. He still wasn't used to it. "So, now?" Bird or no, he was frankly fidgeting now.

She grinned at him.

"They've not changed that much, bird. And neither have I. There will always be battlefields ...."

Badb's Song
by Stephanie Woodfield

"Over his head is shrieking
A lean hag, quickly hopping,
Over the points of their weapons and shields.
She is the grey-haired Morrigu."
Book of Leinster

    A chorus sings below me. Throaty cries ring out, shouts and the clashing of shield and sword. The power of the fray spirals up on the air. It caresses black feathers. I sore higher and higher, following the call of battle frenzy, and the smell of mingled blood and sweat to those who whisper, shout, and scream my name. Blood spills upon the ground, life ebbs and flows. They sacrifice their lives so easily, so willingly, so wastefully. Some to protect those they love, some for valor, ideals, others for pettiness and greed. I drink it all in, the sweet and the bitter. I am all of it, the frenzy, the battle madness, the power behind what makes men stand defiant. I make them remember some things are worth dying for.

    When all is done, when all is quiet, my feet touch the ground. Feathers become pale flesh, talons nimble feet. I am a shadow upon the battlefield. My fingers brush cold skin, weaving moonlight, unbinding spirit from husk. Over shields and weapons I glide, gathering the dead as spirits rise from ruined flesh like morning mist. If not for I, who would care for the dead? What god has the stomach for it? Who would guide spirits and shades to rest, who will wash the bloody armor clean and bring the soul to rebirth, if not for I? Birth and death are both a bloody thing, but I was never one to turn my head away from an un-pretty truth.

    A crooning sound escapes my lips, and I sing. "Your tether to life I unbind, your fate I unwind, so in my halls this night you will dine ...." I sing, and sing, of life and death and all that is in between, and spirits gather. They will call me the spirit of war, the crow of battle, and they will fear me. But I am the one who makes life sweeter by reminding you it will one day end. I am the one who gives you courage when you stand upon the precipice. I am a necessary darkness, a necessary truth.

Ravens
by Diotima Sophia

The women looked over the battlefield. They knew the horrible work before them, they'd done it too many times before – if not them, then their sisters, their mothers, their grandmothers .... Moving forward, they disturbed flocks of black birds, whose cries sounded loud above them.
They bent to their tasks, but few shed tears. There were few left to shed. Too much had happened in their lives already, to weep now.

They were none of them young. The young women had been the spoils of war for the victors, and were now either slaves marking behind the horde, or dead from mistreatment. Not that all the older ones had escaped that fate; age and position meant nothing once their men were defeated; they counted as less than nothing. Old, crippled, terrified, many of them had still fallen to drunken soldiers.

But the victors had moved on, and "at least they didn't burn the village", as the wise woman had said. And it was true, thought Acha, they had not; probably hadn't seen the point. The men were dead (or as good as – any who had fled the battle would be back), the children had either been killed or taken with their mothers (the girls, mostly – their fates were clear). There were only the old women left, now.

And so they moved onto the battlefield.

Those they could recognise as their own, they would burn. As a group, they preferred to bury their dead, but what strength they had, they would conserve for the fields; and the men were dead anyway, what would they care?

There were things to be gathered from the battlefield as well: the victors had been better equipped than the men of the village and so had taken little from the fallen. But the weapons left, the water carriers, even the boots, might be needed in the days and months to come.

They'd wrapped their lower faces in cloth, to keep out the worst of the smell. But the battle had been days ago; they'd not dared to go to the field till the army was well away. Nothing could keep out the stench. Or the sight. Few would sleep this night.

But then, Acha thought, who had been sleeping, anyway? Before the battle, preparations and worry had kept them up. Since the battle .... They had all been mothers. Who could sleep through the screams of children?

Yet now, the children were all gone, and there was work to do. She bent down yet again, removing boots, gathering weapons, dragging what was left of bodies to the pyre. By twilight, it was done. The field was clear of bodies and of anything salvageable.

"When you come down to it," Acha said, looking back, "it's not that big a field. It's not that big a pyre, either, considering it's ruined so many lives, and consigned us all to starvation this winter."

"Has it?" The voice came from behind her. Acha knew the speaker; after all, for all that it was now quiet, this was still a battlefield.

"Has it not, Lady? We are few to feed, yes, but the crops require more work than we can give. None of us can hunt; we will have no meat this winter but what we find already dead, if we can stave off the birds. We'll work, we'll plant and reap – and we will die."

The woman in white responded, "All do, eventually."

Acha looked at her, at this woman she knew the others would not see, and finally asked, her hand moving to take in all around them, "Did it have to happen?"

She was repaid for her question, as she knew she would be, by laughter rather than sympathy. "Few things have to happen. But this has happened, and can not be changed." The woman regarded Acha. "But still, you asked. This took courage."

The woman looked around her, around them. Most of the rest of the women had gone back to the village; they would light the pyre another night.

"What would you ask of me?"

Acha considered her answer carefully, and then, with slumping shoulders, replied, "Peace, Lady. I ask not life, but let us die, as we will soon enough, in peace. Hold them" (she pointed to the ravens even now flocking on the pyre), "off until the last of us is gone."

The Lady looked to her birds, and back to Acha.

"So be it." She raised her hand, and the ravens dispersed to the winds.

But Acha knew, as she trailed back to the village that night, that they would return one day. Ravens are forever hungry.

Rituals, Prayers, and Recipes

The Morrighan
by Katy de Haviland

How to Build an Altar to the Morrigan
by Rebecca Buchanan

Begin with a feather,
black,
but iridescent,
shimmering purple-blue
when you spin it in the light.

Next, a candle;
white is best,
for bones and teeth and purity.

And a bowl;
for blood,
you may think.

Yes,
but more:
into the bowl
spill your fear,
your anxiety, your bitterness,
memories of betrayal and panic,
the ache of self-loathing.

Sacrifice
your weaknesses,
that which makes you less.

Offer them to Her,
a feast for the Raven
who gorges on dead things
leaving only the vital and the strong.

Morrigan Altar
By Blackbird O'Connell

Prayer to the Morrigan
by Galina Krasskova

I call You,
Supreme War goddess.
I call You,
Battle Raven,
I call You,
Terror of men
and Washer at the ford of fate,
and I bow my head before You.

Oh You Who stalk the battlefield,
feast upon our fears
as a hound upon the battle's fallen.
Drive us, ancient Warrior,
Goddess of battles,
of terror, and hope, and power,
drive us into truth.
Drive us into integrity.
Drive us until we have no choice
but to be as the Gods meant us to be,
without apology.

Hail to You, Morrigan.
Hail, Mother of Battle.
Hail to the victories You bring.

Prayer to the Morrigan for Blessing
by Morgan Daimler

Morrigan, battle Queen,
Give me the gift of relentlessness
That I might turn and turn and return
Let my will be like
An eel, a wolf, a hornless heifer,
An old woman seeking blessing
To turn my enemies' blows to healing
May I be strong in serving my purpose
Sharp as a blade's edge
Wise as the crow who sees
The entire battlefield from above
Bless me, Queen of Phantoms,
With all these qualities
In your name and in your service

Invocation of Morrigu
by Morgan Daimler

I call to you,
Daughter of Ernmas,
Sister of battle and sovereignty,
I call to you
Goddess of war-craft,
victory, and death
I call to you Great Queen
Morrigu, Lady of Phantoms
Be with me now

Prayer to An Morrigan
by Blackbird O'Connell

Great Queen Morrígan
Please grant me nerves of steel
A swift fist, Sharp vision
Calm demeanor, Quick mind
And the courage to represent you
In thought, word and deed.
Through your strength anything
Is possible.

Prayer to the Morrigan for Protection
by Morgan Daimler

Great Goddess, Morrigan
May your strong shield be between
myself and all harm and danger
May your sharp sword be between
myself and all who would attack me
May your magical skill be between
myself and all ill-will and ill-wishing
Morrigan, Great Goddess
May your protection be on me
  today, tomorrow, and forever
  today, tomorrow, and forever

Morrigan Prayer
by Sophie Reicher

Lady of Power, cast Your Raven wings over me.
Dark Lady of Battles, turn Your face against my enemies.
Fierce Destroyer, Goddess of warriors,
Protect Your warrior here.
Please Shield me with Your strength,
that I may triumph in my work for You.
Hail to You, Terrible One.
Who brings victory via ordeal.
Hail to You, Hungry for Battle,
Who grants no quarter.
Hail to You, Implacable One.
Hail, Morrigan.

Song to the Morrigan
by Morgan Daimler

Queen of Phantoms,
Blood soaked earth
and rushing river ford
are your domain
Your gifts are madness,
death, and battle-frenzy
You appear, dancing
from sword point
to shield rim,
I sing to you with
a crow's voice, shrieking
I sing to you with
strength and anger

Queen of Nightmares
The joining of rivers
and deep delving caves
are your domain
Your gifts are prophecy,
destruction, or victory
You appear, washing
the clothes of the doomed,
red with gore,
I sing to you with
a voice of blood, crimson
I sing to you with
pain and sorrow

Great Queen
The boiling whirlpool
and fertile field
are your domain
Your gifts are sovereignty,
success, and victory
You appear, offering
your blessing to those
willing to pay the price
I sing to you with
a wolf's voice, howling
I sing to you with
passion and purpose

Samhain Invocation for The Morrigan
by Adrian Barlow

Hail the Battle Raven
The Phantom Queen
The Goddess of Sovereignty
Mistress of Magic
And
Fairy Queen

Hail the Morrigan
Triform Goddess
Blessed Macha, Badb, and Nau
Keeper of the Cauldron
Singing of Fate

On the night of the thinnest veil
We, your children, do call on you
Hear us, we sing your praise
See us, we dance in your praise
Bless us all

Dragon's blood burnt as an offering
Red candles aflame in the dark night
Mighty Morrigan, come and join us
On this Samhain Night

A Prayer to The Morrigan
by Judith O'Grady

Lend me Your Midnight Wings, Goddess!
Help me to fly,
Out of the Land and into the Sky.

Wrap me in Your Black Wings, Goddess!
Help me to rest,
Safe and secure by no storms distressed.

Morrigan Warrior Queen
by Sara Star

An Invocation to The Morrigan
by Judith O'Grady

Hear and attend, O Goddess of Black!
I speak, to whom You have often spoken.
Come with a murder of crows at your back,
Let the bond between us be unbroken.

In your dark heart, will You restore me?
An unkindness of ravens flies ahead;
I feel your hands behind, before me,
I hear your voice inside my head.

You who spoke words of foretelling;
Gall fills my cup and overflows.
Let it be with honey welling,
Carry me up, O Holy Crows!

Reclaiming Power with the Morrigan
by David Salisbury

Is the Morrigan a death goddess? A battle goddess? A goddess of prophecy and vision? Or does she rule the broad powers of sovereignty altogether in all its forms? In a way, all of them are right and none of them are right. For she is all those things are more. The Morrigan is seen as the screaming hag who rides into battle to carry the souls of the deceased. It is she who appears as the bleak and black storm clouds that gather over the horizon before the settling in of our greatest struggles. She is also the raven, the muscular bird of wonder and dread, screeching in the chill night.

What do all of those associations have in common? To me the linking thread can be summed up in one word: power. Power is the driving force of all civilization. It is what we crave when we reach adulthood and what so many feel they lack when they find themselves on the edge of death. Whether it is power of the self (sovereignty) or power over others, power is the cup of life for which we all thirst. Probably one of the most loaded words in the entire lexicon of human language, power can be healing or crippling, preserving or destructive. Like the gathering storm of the Morrigan, it is the wind that generates our electricity currents or topples over our buildings in the hurricane.

To the devotee of the Morrigan, issues of power are both complex and heartfelt. The oppression that so many people face in areas considered both "civilized" and not make some people loath establishments that hoard power and the resources it garners. For those people, the Morrigan becomes a symbol of liberation and freedom, a source of hope and reclaiming of independence for a future where we can all operate under the ownership of our individual expressions. The raven, seen as her prime animal form, is not shy about expressing its cries to the unsuspecting passerby. They operate in groups, yet each bird also has its own unique character traits. Recent studies even show that ravens and crows can actually remember the faces of humans they encounter as a method of protection and communication to their fellow birds. In this way, the raven not only expresses its own sovereignty and power, but it recognizes those gifts in others, as well.

There is a valuable lesson to be learned here. Once we can claim our own power and recognize the power in others, we can begin to work in the world in a way that serves our will and the will of the gods in the most efficient ways possible. When we stand up and tell the world that we have plenty of power -- power enough to share -- then everyone has enough. And when everyone has enough power, there is little need for struggle and strife. Sound like an ideal hippie fantasy? It may be, but that doesn't mean it's altogether impossible either. Think of it this way: when I extend my hand outward to shake your hand, you are likely to return the gesture. Whether from a sense of societal obligation or a feeling of trust and camaraderie, you still give that gesture back to me. Why is that? Because I just expressed my ability [power] to reach out, to make a connection. Power is about making connections and doing something with them. After all, many will say that as a goddess of the ever-shifting spiritual realms, the Morrigan has the power to make connections with the souls of the living and the dead. Using these connections, she can lead the way to the lands of shadow and mist, beyond the veil of time and reason. She has access to the powers of the Here and the Great Beyond, and so can we.

Much of this connective power has been lost over the years. Blame it on the fall of polytheism from the world or the general disconnection that human beings tend to have with each other on intimate levels. Either way, we like to think that only our own power matters. And not even everybody believes in their own power, anyway. But for those who do, we have a real chance at getting some of that power back every day. The following simple rite does just that.

Materials Needed:

A cup of clean water
Coarse or finely ground salt (regular sea salt or himalayan)
One red candle

This rite is especially useful when performed on the dark of the moon, that time just slightly before the moon starts to wax, or increase in its size and power. When tied to the moon, we can tether ourselves to its power and siphon some of its rich magick for our own.

Have all the materials before you, and a cleansed and consecrated space. It would be appropriate to bathe or at least be relatively clean before the actual working of the rite. Having your physical body be cleansed of actual dirt and grime means there's more room for strength and power to fill your being. In any case, being "properly prepared" (as the magic-worker is famous for saying) for the operation is important.

Gather around yourself your own lifeforce energy. Ground, and soak in the cool sovereign powers of the earth. Feel those powers encircle your physical form, then the etheric, and finally the "godsoul" or whatever you view as your highest form. Extend your arms out and raise them high above you. Call out to the Morrigan with these words or similar words of your own choosing:

> "Cool earth affirms the shade of your presence.
> Midnight Queen, song of the raven, witness this rite.
> Under the dark of the moon and on the edge of the
> water's gift, I make my blessing."

Light the red candle. Trace a star of any numbered points above the cup of water. Sprinkle three pinches of salt into the cup of water. Infuse it with the energy that you summoned up from the depths of the earth. Once again raise your arms:

> "Water is the gift of life, the hidden cleansing glory of the raging storm.
> Storm Queen, you of the lightning hag's shrieking cry, witness this rite.
> With the cup of the Old Ones, I reclaim the gifts of my personal authority."

Once again trace a star over the cup. This time, repeat the star-tracing process several times, going faster and faster until you reach a blurring speed, slowing down shortly after you reach the height of that speed. Slowly raise the cup to your mouth as you whisper "Power, I take it back. Power, I take it back." Then drink the cup down all at once.

You can then either leave the candle burning or let it burn out. I like to leave it burning safely for the duration of the night, but of course do this only at your own risk.

The water rite above calls upon the "storm rider" aspect of the Morrigan, asking her to gift you with the powerful water that a deeply cleansing rainstorm gives. With water being connected to the ebb and flow of the moon and the power of the tides, you align yourself with increasing strength and vitality. The rite can be performed either once a month on every dark moon or with whatever frequency you feel is needed to stand confidently in full power.

With the Morrigan, we have a fantastic opportunity to step back through time from our various stages of life and reclaim what was lost to us. We reclaim power, but with that we also reclaim compassion, individuality, and our very essence. So take the cup of life from the Queen of Storms and start living life to the full height of your power. The Morrigan would surely accept nothing less.

Source of Enchantments:
A Devotional Rite of the Morrigan
by L. Sixfingers

The following is a modern devotional rite to the Mórrígan, including trance elements and divinatory work. The purpose of this rite is to continue to build and honor your relationship with the Mórrígan and create a ritual space to consult Her wisdom and gain Her blessings. The rite is meant to be a framework for your practice with plenty of space for innovation and individualization.

Perform this rite at the dark of the moon when the night is deepest and Her power churns through the land.

In addition to any images of the Mórrígan, or other items you regularly keep on your altar, you should have:
*A central altar candle
*Incense
*At least three beautiful beads for the Ravens
*A dish, bowl, or box specifically to hold the beads for the Ravens
*At least two Raven feathers
*A vessel of water – this can be still water or water infused with sacred oils and herbs
*Sacred herbs such as Juniper, Vervain, Hawthorn, and Mugwort
*A special offering to the Mórrígan

Begin by taking nine centering breaths, deep inhalations and complete exhalations that focus the mind and call all parts of yourself home to be present for the rite. Perform any rites of shielding and warding you may have if that is part of your practice.

Take to one knee, if able, and recite:
>I am bending my knee
>In the eye of the Mother who created me,
>In the eye of the Maiden who loves me,
>In the eye of the Crone who guides me,
>>In friendship and affection.
>Through Thine gift of grace, O Goddess,
>Bestow upon us fullness in our need,
>>Love towards Goddess,
>>The affection of Goddess,
>>The smile of Goddess,
>>The wisdom of Goddess,
>>The passion of Goddess,
>>The hope of Goddess,
>>And the will of Goddess,
>To do in the world of the Nine Queens
>As ancestors and ageless ones
>Do in-between;
>>Each shade and light
>>Each day and night,
>>Each time in kindness,
>>Give Thou us Thy Spirit.(1)

Ring the bell nine times to wake the temple within, without, and between: three times below, three times above, and three times before you. The sound also dissipates all that would cause harm and welcomes your guides from the three worlds. To bless the space say:

>May all who enter in this space,
>do so only by Her grace.

Light your altar candle. Next you will be reciting your Name Poem, announcing yourself, stating your lineage and skills. If you do not have a Name Poem, take time before this ritual to write one. A Name Poem may be as simple as stating your Name (magickal, given, or both) maybe with a mention of your biological and/or spiritual heritage. It may also be more elaborate, stating your skills, your accomplishments, the community you come from, and the God/desses you serve. The following is an example of a Name Poem:

>I am Éxtasis
>Beloved of the Mórrígan
>Granddaughter of Ernmas and Ix Chel
>I break sorceries of hate
>And cast enchantments of empowerment
>I walk bravely through all the worlds
>I bear scars of battle and scars of love
>May I ever be full of honor
>May I ever speak with truth
>May I ever by one of the Mórrígan's Raven Children

Once you have spoken your Name Poem and presented yourself in the rite, it is time to make offering to Earth, Sea, and Sky. Begin with Earth. Holding up your offering of sacred herbs, say:

>Powers of the Earth that is Her body
>I give to you
>You give to me
>Sustained and whole
>Blessed be!

If you are outside, offer your sacred herbs directly to the Earth. If you are indoors, reserve the herbs on your altar until you can offer them to the Earth after the rite.

Next, make your offering to the Sea. Hold up your water offering and say:

> Powers of the Sea that is Her blood
> I give to you
> You give to me
> Sustained and whole
> Blessed be!

If you are outside, offer your water directly to the Earth. If you are indoors, reserve the water on the altar until you can offer them to the Earth after the rite.

Finally, make your offering to the Sky. Light your incense and say:

> Powers of the Sky that is Her breath
> I give to you
> You give to me
> Sustained and whole
> Blessed be!

Offer the incense to any images of the Mórrígan you may have on your altar and let it burn for the remainder of the rite.

Next, we will give offering to the Ravens, Mórrígan's beloved creatures of the sky, who will help guide us to Her Realm Between where we can perform our divination. Show them your offering of beads – I usually offer three at a time, eventually having enough beads to create a necklace to wear in their honor.(2) Hold the beads up and say:

Ravens
All-knowing
Morrighan's Messengers
Watching from the Tree
Brush your wings across my shoulders
Guide me through the mists with your cries!

Take up your Raven feather(s) and begin to brush them across your shoulders in a sweeping rhythm. You are beginning the process of moving 'tween the worlds and when you are ready, recite the chant to induce trance.(3) Begin your recitation slowly, eventually picking up speed, following the cries of the Ravens beyond the mists to the realm of the Mórrígan.

Dark Moon
Red Wound
Deep Tide
Endless Sky
Sucks in
Spits out
Moon face
Turned about
Black Maiden
Old Crone
Wrap me in
Moon blood and bone

As the mists part, slow you recitation of the chant until you have fully arrived at your destination.

Now 'tween the worlds, it is time to invoke the Great Queen, the Mórrígan. You may invoke Her in a way that is familiar to you, or you can use the following text from the *Lebor Gabála Erenn* or *Book of Invasions*. I have provided both the Gaelic and English versions:

> Heriu cid rotbla roa
> Banba Fotla & Fea
> Nemaind nar fodaind fathaig
> Donand mathair na ndea.
>
> Badb is Macha mét indbais
> Morrígan. Fotla felbais.
> indelma ind ága ernmais.
> ingena ána Ernmais.
>
> Eriu – where is it that the famous road proceeded? –
> Banba, Fotla & Fea
> Nemain of the prophetic stanzas
> Danu, Mother of the Gods.
>
> Badb and Macha, greatness of wealth,
> Morrigan – source of enchantments,
> servants in her attendance,
> were the daughters of Ernmas.(4)

Greet the Mórrígan and hold up the offering you have prepared for Her. Next, recite the following to invoke the blessings of the Mórrígan. Her blessing is the final preparation before your divination to seek wisdom from Her guidance. It is also a blessing of you as the Mórrígan -- as we are Her and She is us.

> Mórrígan Mórrígan Mórrígan
> May I see Your dark-bright face
> Mórrígan Mórrígan Mórrígan
> May I hear Your red-mouth song
> Mórrígan Mórrígan Mórrígan
> May I feel Your fierce-love touch
> Mórrígan Mórrígan Mórrígan
> May I taste Your nine-fold wisdom
> Mórrígan Mórrígan Mórrígan
> May I know your every way
> Mórrígan Mórrígan Mórrígan

With your chosen divinatory tool ask the question you have of the Mórrígan. When completed, give thanks, hold up again your offering and begin the return through the mists. Call to the Raven guides:

> Through the mists I return
> I hear the Ravens calling me home
> Through the mists I return
> Back to body, blood, and bone

Again, recite this chant repeatedly, this time at a continuous slow and steady beat until you arrive back through the mists.

Once you have returned, take time to properly ground and center. End with thanks and blessings. I recite an adaption of the Badb's peace prophecy to end the rite:

> Peace to sky,
> sky to earth,
> be this nine time eternal.

Notes

Adaptation of a traditional prayer from the *Carmina Gadelica*. Carmichael, Alexander. *Carmina Gadelica: Hymns and Incantations from the Gaelic*. Aurora, CO: Lindisfarne Press, 1992. Print.

Thanks to Lupa (http://www.thegreenwolf.com/) for the offering-to-necklace inspiration.

Trance is a skill that takes time and practice to develop. To deepen your experience of this rite and any ecstatic ritual, I would encourage you to study trancework. Resources such as Diana Paxson's *Tranceportation: Learning to Navigate the Inner World* are immensely useful. The Ravens will especially appreciate your effort.

Macalister, Robert Alexander Stewart, trans. *Lebor Gabála Erenn*. Dublin: Irish Texts Society, 1938. 217. Print.

Morrighan's Flight
by Alexis J Money

Invocation of the Morrighan Ritual
Dark of the Moon
by Shea Morgan

The purpose of this ritual is to bodily invoke the Morrighan as a devotional act and to receive messages from her for yourself; and, if done in a circle setting, for those in the circle. This ritual may be performed with your own circle casting, and may also include any version of the Great Rite in token prior to the Invocation of the Morrighan.

As with any invocation, it is best to have done your research, meditated, and worked with the deity in advance. Offerings are always a good idea, and I prefer offerings of red wine outdoors in nature. The Morrighan courted me for several months prior to the first invocation, during which time I undertook several journeys with her to test my readiness.

As preparation for the ritual, I made a collage candle of symbols sacred to her and our journey together. I wore nine red tresses in my hair, used red candles, black altar clothes, and black crystals.

A year and a day after this invocation during a coven ceremony, she became my Matron in a shamanic journey to the Underworld. Her blessings are many, and I will never forget the first invocation. It resides in my heart, as does the Morrighan.

I: Circle Casting

A: Quarter Calls

Hail Guardian of the Watchtower of the North
Element of Earth and the Crystal Kingdom
Grace, beauty and power of the Horse
Intuition, cunning and strength of the Wolf
Guide us on our journey tonight and in the future

We ask you to attend our circle and guard the gate.
Hail and Welcome!

All: Hail and Welcome!

Hail Guardian of the Watchtower of the East
Element of Air and the Feathered Kingdom
Mystery, magick and insight of the Raven
Splendor, practicality and resourcefulness of the Vulture
Guide us on our journey tonight and in the future
We ask you to attend our circle and guard the gate.
Hail and Welcome!

All: Hail and Welcome!

Hail Guardian of the Watchtower of the South
Element of Fire and the Kingdom of Flames
Protection, majesty and wisdom of the Dragon
Transformation, steadfastness and beauty of the Phoenix
Guide us on our journey tonight and in the future
We ask you to attend our circle and guard the gate.
Hail and Welcome!

All: Hail and Welcome!

Hail Guardian of the Watchtower of the West
Element of Water and the Kingdom of Waves
Power, stealth and intuition of the Black Panther
Regeneration, projection and knowing of the Scorpion
Guide us on our journey tonight and in the future
We ask you to attend our circle and guard the gate.
Hail and Welcome!

All: Hail and Welcome!

II: Call to the Morrighan

Hail to The Morrighan! Phantom
Queen! Goddess of Fate! Bestower of Sovereignty!
Goddess with many faces, many guises – yet all one
A drumbeat, a heartbeat, a thread through the ages
Callieach, Earth Goddess, Great Mother, and Crone
Epona, Divine Horse Goddess
Rhiannon, Divine Queen, white horse swift of foot,
Mystic Goddess of Death and Rebirth
Macha, Gatherer of Warriors,
Champion of Women, holder of the key to the Mysteries
You are the Earth Goddess connecting us to the land,
You are the Horse Goddess guiding us on our journeys through life and the Otherworld
You are the Goddess of Death and Rebirth, leading us through the fire of the inner mysteries
We honor you, and we call on you to walk with us
Guide and protect our circle tonight on this dark moon.
Do not fear her, as she is Goddess of the Witches and we are all her daughters/sons;
Hail and Welcome!

III: Call to the Daghda

Hail Daghda! The Good God! Tribal
God! Protector!
You are the All Father, provider to all with your cauldron of life
Food, sustenance, yet also inspiration, ever turning
We ask you for the gift of your wisdom, to bring us balance
Lend your club and shield
Protect and defend us during these rites and in life
We call on you to attend our circle and walk with us.
Hail and Welcome!

All: Hail and Welcome!

IV: Alignment with the Dark of the Moon

Tonight we embrace the darkness. It holds the thought of all to be – all that is within the blackness. It wraps us like a warm cloak of memory and whispers of the future. We journey tonight knowing that we are safe. That the Dark Mother holds us close to her, and the God protects us with his shield. We are safe to enter the mystery and to learn what the Dark Goddess has to teach us.

We welcome their presence in our circle and in our lives and know that each will lead us gently to what we are ready to be shown. We honor them tonight at the Dark of the Moon.
Blessed be.

All: Blessed be.

V: Great Rite

A: Alignment with the Dark Goddess

(Note: if in a group setting, each may speak a line or paragraph and pass around the staff as each speaks a verse)

Howl of the Wolf crying out warning in the darkness
Crackling of the Oak snapping above the roar of the fire
Mushrooms finding life in the crevices of the rotting wood
Naked Birch beckoning us forth with her white fingers of bone

The Dark Lady calls us through the skeletal forest
The land walks in shadows, hiding in dampness and fog

The Hunted now at rest beneath layers of decaying leaves
Crows dancing on the brittle air in a language all their own

Depths of the ocean stillness belied by the crashing waves
Pounding the shoreline, the elements converge
Edge of the deep, water meeting air, shaping the earth
Burning with fire, we walk this path between

She shines her light through her crimson eyes for those that would follow
She calls her children to her side, together, yet we walk this path alone
Courage to hear the warmth under the screech of her cry
Warmth to those brave enough to enter her cloak

We find her there, underneath the mask, if we dare to seek
Heart beating and pulsing together with our own
The Crone, the Hag, the Magick of the Underworld at her command
She holds out the Key in her rot covered hand – will we take it, she asks?

Key to unlock the secrets of the below, of the depths and of our soul.
The secrets of the Apple and its seeds, sweet, yet poison
Datura, whispering, calls us, intoxicating scent of attraction
The Lady has her ways and wiles; her gifts are many

Who will be brave enough to take her gifts when offered?
Where shall they bring you? Her demands are simple though not easy
She asks a path of service in return.
Will you accept her hand now, and the key that has been offered?

B: Alignment with the Morrighan

Morrighan, Great Queen! Phantom Queen! Collector of Souls!
Crows cry in the darkening skies, seeking the spoils of battle
Wolves circle in the hidden depths of the between, devouring carcasses of the remains
Horse tears across the land racing to the battle, fearing nothing under your guiding hand
They announce your presence in our midst
All bow low to the Queen, power beyond measure
Flames rolling forth from Her eyes, clearing the land of all that has served its usefulness
We stand in awe of your might, do you dare to take up Her sword?
Blessed be.

All: Blessed be.

C: Invocation Call to the Morrighan

(Note: This is an invocation with the Fire Pentagram drawn with Wand either by the person who will be invoking the Morrighan or by another Priest/ess who directs the energy of the invoking fire pentagram to the one who will be invoking her.)

Oh Mighty Morrighan!
Great Mother! Protector! Guide!
Patroness of Priestesses and Witches!
Come on your Chariot or Swift of Horse!
I call thee forth!
We quake in your presence
Yet feel your nearness in silent ecstasy
Come closer still, closer still, and closer again
Magick Incarnate! Shapeshifter!

Prophetess!
I seek to join with you
To give myself to you tonight, in this circle
To learn from you and your wisdom
To gain empowerment, intuition and understanding
To drink more deeply of your mysteries
To hear the messages you have to impart
I seek to be a worthy vessel for your presence
To feel your breath against my neck
To feel your caress upon my heart
To feel your heart beating with mine
To feel your touch beside my soul
Be with me, join me, be one with me
I call thee thrice
Morrighan, Morrighan, Morrighan
Come unto me, I invoke thee!
So mote it be!

(Note: Working continues until it reaches its natural conclusion or until it is determined that the work is complete.)

VI: Devocation of the Morrighan

A: Banishing the Fire Pentagram with Wand

We devoke your divine presence from your daughter/son (name of invokee)
We thank you Goddess of the Witches as your daughter/son.
Gently depart our sister/brother, wholly and completely.
May there always be peace between us.

Morrighan, I thank you
For your wisdom
For your understanding
For your mere presence

And as I called unto you,
I now bid you farewell
We are no longer joined
We are no longer one
With gratitude that words cannot speak
I devoke you, wholly and completely
I thank you for the honor of your presence tonight and in my life.
So mote it be!

B: Farewell to the Daghda

Hail Daghda! The Good God! Tribal
God! Protector!
You are the All Father, provider to all with your cauldron of life
Food, sustenance, yet also inspiration, ever turning
We thank you for the gift of your wisdom, bringing us balance
For lending your club and shield and
Protecting and defending us during these rites and in life
We thank you for attending our circle and walking with us.
Hail and Farewell!

All: Hail and Farewell!

C: Farewell to the Morrighan

Hail to The Morrighan! Phantom Queen! Goddess of Fate!
Bestower of Sovereignty!
Goddess with many faces, many guises – yet all one
A drumbeat, a heartbeat, a thread through the ages
Callieach, Earth Goddess, Great Mother and Crone
Epona, Divine Horse Goddess
Rhiannon, Divine Queen, white horse swift of foot, Mystic Goddess of Death and Rebirth

Macha, Gatherer of Warriors, Champion of Women, holder of the key to the Mysteries
You are the Earth Goddess connecting us to the land,
You are the Horse Goddess guiding us on our journeys through life and the Otherworld
Finally, you are the Goddess of Death and Rebirth, leading us through the fire of the inner mysteries
We thank you for walking with us as we honored you this evening
We thank you for guiding and projecting our circle tonight on this dark moon.
Hail and Farewell!

All: Hail and Farewell!

VII: Release of Quarters

Hail Guardian of the Watchtower of the North
Element of Earth and the Crystal Kingdom
Grace, beauty and power of the Horse
Intuition, cunning and strength of the Wolf
Thank you for guiding us on our journey tonight and in the future
Thank you for attending our circle and guarding the gate.
Hail and Farewell!

All: Hail and Farewell!

Hail Guardian of the Watchtower of the West
Element of Water and the Kingdom of Waves
Power, stealth and intuition of the Black Panther
Regeneration, projection and knowing of the Scorpion
Thank you for guiding us on our journey tonight and in the future

Thank you for attending our circle and guarding the gate.
Hail and Farewell!
All: Hail and Farewell!

Hail Guardian of the Watchtower of the South
Element of Fire and the Kingdom of Flames
Protection, majesty and wisdom of the Dragon
Transformation, steadfastness and beauty of the Phoenix
Thank you for guiding us on our journey tonight and in the future
Thank you for attending our circle and guarding the gate.
Hail and Farewell!

All: Hail and Farewell!

Hail Guardian of the Watchtower of the East
Element of Air and the Feathered Kingdom
Mystery, magick and insight of the Raven
Splendor, practicality and resourcefulness of the Vulture
Thank you for guiding us on our journey tonight and in the future
Thank you for attending our circle and guarding the gate.
Hail and Farewell!

All: Hail and Farewell!

(Note: close with a release/casting out of the circle.)

Dedication Ritual to An Morrígan
by Blackbird O'Connell

Tools:
3 candles (with matches)
- 1 for Land Spirits
- 1 for Ancestors
- 1 for *An Morrígan*

1 clean plate for offerings:
- 1 piece of bread
- 1 piece of raw meat

1 clean empty bowl
1 cup of mead
1 Morrígan Pendant

Arrange the candles with the selected *An Morrígan* candle in the center of the other two.

I: OPENING

(lighting the first candle)
I call to the Land Spirits. Through your nourishment and beauty you give me the focus to see the Truth and to reflect that in all that I do.

(pour a little mead into the bowl)
If you so choose I invite you to be my guest in this dedication.

(lighting the second candle)
I call to the Ancestors. Through my veins your blood flows, giving me the courage to always say what is right and tell the Truth even when others do not.

(pour a little mead into the bowl)
If you so choose I invite you to be my guest in this dedication.

(lighting the *An Morrígan* candle)
Great Queen Morrígan, I reach out to you as I dedicate myself to your patronage. Through your actions I always know what I should do to reflect the Truth you bestow upon me.

(pour a little mead in the bowl)

If you so choose, I invite you to be my guest in this dedication. Through these three great flames the light of life is sustained. Failte!

(take a sip of the mead then place it back down)

II: STATEMENT OF PURPOSE

An Morrígan, you are the embodiment of power, courage, honor, and integrity. Through your own steadfast dedication you delivered the blood of Indech mac De Domnann, thus helping to win the Battle of Moytura. You have challenged many warriors to accomplish greatness as you challenge me everyday. You are the Raven Warrior, You are the Great Queen, and I thank you for blessing me with your patronage.

Today I once again align myself with you. From childhood, you guided me without my knowing and you strengthen my every step with your guidance. Years ago you revealed your beauty and bestowed Blackbird upon me. Every day you offer your protective guard, inspiring me to stay strong and remain diligent, always putting honor and Truth above all else.

(hold the Morrígan pendant over the Morrígan flame)

    I dedicate myself to you on this day as I do every Samhain. Through you anything is possible and because of you I adhere to the motto of the Fianna - Fírinne inár gcroithibh, neart inár lámhaibh, agus comhall inár dteangthaibh.

(remove pendant from flame and let it cool)

III: OFFERING

(picking up the bread from the plate)
I share this offering of food and drink with you as gifts in hope that you will recognize that I come to you pure of heart, and, if you see fit, help guide and protect me on my journey in this life.

(takes a piece of the bread off and eats it)
I dedicate myself to *An Morrígan* and honor all three flames upholding and exemplifying the Truth which they reveal to me.

(pour what is left of the mead into the bowl)

IV: CLOSING

(turning to the Land Spirits candle)

Though I blow out this candle it does not extinguish the flame that lights up in my eyes when I glance out at the beauty of the land around me. Go raibh maith agat agus slán abhaile!

(blows out the land spirits candle)

(turn to the ancestors candle)

Though I blow out this candle it does not extinguish the flame in my heart where in me pumps the blood of those who have come before me. Go raibh maith agat agus slán abhaile!

(blow out the ancestors candle)

(turning to the Morrígan candle)
Though I blow out this candle it does not extinguish the flame in my mind that stores the Truth of your presence in my life. Go raibh maith agat agus slán abhaile!

(blow out the Morrígan candle)

(Place the Morrígan pendant on a chain and wear it at all possible times as a reminder of your shared bond)

Nemain Blessing Amulet
by Sophie Reicher

Over the years, whenever I honored or encountered the Morrigan, I have come to believe that Her primary paths or faces are Badb, Macha, Anu, and Nemain. For all I know, there may be more, but these are the shifting faces She showed to me. While I work mostly for Macha, occasionally I encounter Her other facets, and in one instance, I received the following blessing charm for Nemain.

- Rose buds
- Malva flowers
- Heather (the herb soaked in heather oil, if possible)
- Pepper berries
- Rose oil (in this one instance, synthetic is okay, as real rose oil is terribly expensive)
- Mahogany obsidian
- Small Quartz point
- Lapis lazuli
- Red heart
- Tiger's eye

Put in a pouch of midnight blue.

All of the ingredients should be carefully acquired, mindful of how they were mined or grown. They should be brought to Nemain's altar and given into Her care to be blessed for the full turning of a moon. Then, on the night of the dark moon, assembled into a pouch. It may be carried or worn to invoke Her protection.

Badb Amulet
by Sophie Reicher

Leather bag
Heather
Dittany
Big red rose
One black tourmaline
One small amethyst ball

Again, as with the amulet to Nemain, the ingredients should be carefully gathered and given to Badb on Her altar for Her to bless. They should be allowed to sit there for the full turning of the moon and then, whenever you feel ready, assembled into an amulet. If you are in service to the Morrigan, particularly if you are in service to Badb, a few drops of your own blood, carefully drawn with a diabetic lancet, may be added to the pouch. It may then be worn to invoke Her blessings.

Morrigan Incense
by Galina Krasskova

Base:
2 tonka beans
2 tsp. juniper
2 tsp cypress
3 tps pathchouli.
Pulverize in a blender.

Add
2 tsp. dragonsblood
4-5 crushed bay leaves
1 ½ tsp orris powder
1 tsp rosemary,
1 tsp ground clove,
2 tsp heather that has been soaked in a capful of musk oil and allowed to dry.
Grind this all together.

Store with a whole tonka bean. If you are owned by the Morrigan, add a few drops of your own blood.

Morrigan Blessing Oil

Equal parts: ambergris (you may use a synthetic),
dark musk,
tea rose

Morrigan Incense
from Iseum of the Star*Eyed Warrior

½ part acorns, both smashed and whole
¾ parts dragonsblood
¼ part champhor
1 part white sandalwood
½ part mistletoe
¼ part calamus
½ lavender
½ rosemary (strength and courage)
3-4 tonka beans
¼ part poppy seeds
½ bay leaves
½ myhrr
¼ part St. Johnswort (defender)
¼ part cinnamon
½ part Deerstongue
¼ part damiana (sexuality)
½ saw palmetto
¼ part mandrake
¼ cardamom (grind the seeds)
½ ambergris

Morrigan Oil

½ musk
½ rose
touch of patchouli
touch of camphor

Our Contributors

S. E. Acker lives in small-town Missouri where there are more cows than houses with two impossibly bossy dogs, and is a part-time writer with a novel coming out this year through Permuted Press and a full-time Pagan/Dedicant of the Morrigan.

Ophelia Anu has opted not to provide a biography

Adrian Barlow has been a practicing witch going on 15 years; he comes from Irish descent and generations of gypsy blood. He started as a priest of Hekate, until called by The Morrigan and now honours them both. He has spent his life trying to discover the mysteries of the Gods and better understand them.

Christa A. Bergerson is foremost a Guardian of Nature and those who writhe betwixt the gossamer veil. She is also an occultist, an organic master gardener, and in moons to come, she will be a practicing Traditional Chinese Medicine Doctor. For now, she is a Witch Doctor. Her intuitive poetry has appeared in *Abyss & Apex*, *Circle Magazine*, *Waters of Life*, *Lalitamba*, and *Bearing Torches*, among several other publications. For sublunary communication, contact her at carmentaeternus@comcast.net

Frances Billinghurst is an initiated witch and High Priestess of an active coven based in Adelaide, South Australia, as well as Priestess in Residence of The Goddess House. For over 20 years Frances has been interested in the occult and all things magical, as well as folklore, mythology, and ancient cultures. A prolific writer, her articles have appeared in publications including *Llewellyn's Witch's Calendar*, *The Cauldron*, *Unto Herself: A Devotional Anthology to Independent Goddesses*, *A Mantle of Stars:*

A Devotional to the Queen of Heaven, and *The Faerie Queens*. Her own book, *Dancing the Sacred Wheel: A Journey through the Southern Sabbats*, first published in 2012, is due to be re-released later in 2014. When she is not writing, Frances is attempting to replicate the Hanging Gardens of Babylon on her patch of Australian dirt, and journeying between the worlds. More information about Frances can be found on the Temple of the Dark Moon's web site (www.templedarkmoon.com) or The Goddess House blog (thegoddesshouse.blogspot.com.au).

Nicole Bonvisuto is a Universalist navigating through many paths and devotional practices. She is a devotee of Loki who has been blessed by the Morrigan's presence in her life. Faith aside, Nicole has devoted her work to environmental awareness and social justice. She currently lives in Michigan with her husband and a Jack Russell Terrier. Somedays, it is difficult to tell the two apart.

Ashley R. Bryner is a Druid artist dedicated to the Morrighan, and lives in Baltimore, Md. with her husband and two cats. She has created many devotional works over the years, and works as a professional photographer when she is not creating art or running rituals at her local Cedarlight Grove, ADF. She wishes to express her gratitude for the undying support of her loved ones and community.

Rebecca Buchanan is the editor of the Pagan literary ezine *Eternal Haunted Summer*. She is the editor-in-chief of Bibliotheca Alexandrina, and blogs regularly at BookMusings: (Re)Discovering Pagan Literature. She has been previously published in *Cliterature*, *Linguistic Erosion*, *Luna Station Quarterly*, and other venues.

Morgan Daimler is a blogger, poet, teacher of esoteric subjects, Druid, and dedicant of Macha. Her poetry has been published in several anthologies as well as in *Circle Magazine* and *Witches and Pagans Magazine*. She has a self published book called *By Land, Sea, and Sky*, a book of poetry called *Shadow, Light, and Spirit*, and a novel, *Murder Between the Worlds*. Through Spero publishing, she wrote a children's book called *A Child's Eye View of the Fairy Faith,* and through Moon Books she wrote *Where the Hawthorn Grows* and the forthcoming *Fairy Witchcraft*. Morgan blogs for Moon Books, Hartford Faith and Values, as well as her own blog.

Valiel Elentári is a French, hard-polytheist working with Gods and Spirits. She connects with Divine Beings that come close and ask for it, which makes it difficult to summarize her practices. Her main affinities lay with the Norse, Celtic, Greek and Egyptian pantheons; she recognizes all Gods but she does not work with all of them, only specific ones among each pantheons. She's owned by the Morrigan and works the most closely with primal and Death-related deities and spirits, in-between Spirits, and Spirits of the Dead, as her path revolves around seership, thresholds and death work.

Hope Maree Foley is a devoted Priestess of the Morrigan and Initiate of the Shamanic and Naturopathic crafts with a passion for plant magick, herbal medicine and shifting paradigms. Working closely with ancestral knowledge, gnostic connection to land and the scientific method, she seeks syncretism of ecstatic experience and embodied being. She is known for her Warrior spirit, Fey demeanour, and passionate love affair with cacao.

Born on Valencia (Spain), in 1985, **Gebirgsjägerinne** found her path with Morrigan in 2009, when her husband joined the Spanish Mountain Troops. After one year living on the

Pyrennees, she felt the call of duty and now she's trying to be a soldier herself. Her creed is way far from just spirituality, she knows the suffering of the soldier and the cold of the mountains and the wood, and that feels like home in such hard form of living.

Katy de Haviland has opted not provide a biography

Iseum of the Star*Eyed Warrior was founded in 1995 under the auspices of the Fellowship of Isis by Rev. Galina Krasskova. While it was a place of welcome for all Deities, the core focus from the beginning was honoring Goddesses of war and martial power. The Iseum closed formally in 2013.

Galina Krasskova is a polytheist, Heathen, and Northern Tradition shaman. The author of over a dozen books she can generally be found at krasskova.weebly.com lurking and causing trouble.

Saigh Kym Lambert is a Gaelic Heathen dedicated primarily to the Irish War Goddesses. Along with research on these Goddesses and the warriors in Gaelic and Germanic cultures, she combines her ecstatic practice with various forms of physical training. A personal trainer and homesteader, she lives in mountain swamp with a small pack of dogs and a herd of horses, among other beasts including one EMT. Her War Goddess project can be found at Shadow of the Hooded Crow. http://dunsgathan.net/caithream/

Jennifer Lawrence likes doing things the hard way, which explains most of how her life has turned out. She has earned a B.A. in Literature and a B.S. in Criminal Justice. She lives with five cats, and a houseful of gargoyles somewhere outside of Chicago, and has followed the Tuatha Dé Danann (among others) for over twenty-five years. Her interests include history, animal osteology, gardening, herbalism, mythology and fairy tales, hiking, camping, and the martial arts.

Gerri Leen lives in Northern Virginia and originally hails from Seattle. She has a collection of short stories, *Life Without Crows*, out from Hadley Rille Books, and stories and poems published in such places as: *Sword and Sorceress XXIII*, *Spinetinglers*, *Entrances and Exits*, *She Nailed a Stake Through His Head*, *Dia de los Muertos*, *Return to Luna*, *Triangulation: Dark Glass*, *Sails & Sorcery*, and *Paper Crow*. Visit http://www.gerrileen.com to see what else she's been up to.

Hannah Lipsky is a practicing eclectic pagan, by which she means she is practicing very hard in the hopes of one day being good at it. She can most often be found dancing dangerously, playing with swords, or spinning tales by the fire.

P. Sufenas Virius Lupus is a metagender, and the Doctor, Magistratum, Mystagogos, Sacerdos, and one of the founding members of the Ekklesía Antínoou–a queer, Graeco-Roman-Egyptian syncretist reconstructionist polytheist group dedicated to Antinous, the deified lover of the Roman Emperor Hadrian, and related deities and divine figures–as well as a contributing member of Neos Alexandria and a practicing Celtic Reconstructionist pagan in the traditions of gentlidecht and filidecht, as well as Romano-British, Welsh, and Gaulish deity devotions. Lupus is also dedicated to several land spirits around the area of North Puget Sound and its islands. Lupus holds a Ph.D. in Celtic Civilizations from the National University of Ireland/University College Cork. Lupus' work (poetry, fiction, and essays) has appeared in a number of Bibliotheca Alexandrina devotional volumes, as well as Ruby Sara's anthologies *Datura* (2010) and *Mandragora* (2012), Inanna Gabriel and C. Bryan Brown's *Etched Offerings* (2011), Lee Harrington's *Spirit of Desire: Personal Explorations of Sacred Kink*

(2010), and Galina Krasskova's *When the Lion Roars* (2011). Lupus has also written several full-length books, including *The Phillupic Hymns* (2008), *The Syncretisms of Antinous* (2010), *Devotio Antinoo: The Doctor's Notes, Volume One* (2011), *All-Soul, All-Body, All-Love, All-Power: A TransMythology* (2012), *A Garland for Polydeukion* (2012), and *A Serpent Path Primer* (2012), with more on the way. Lupus writes the "Queer I Stand" column at Patheos.com's Pagan Portal, the "Gentlidecht" blog at PaganSquare, and also blogs at Aedicula Antinoi (http://aediculaantinoi.wordpress.com/).

Rufus Brock Maychild has been Pagan for nearly 40 years. He is an ordained Priest in the Fellowship of Isis, founder of the Iseum of Pandora. He works as a Pagan Prison Chaplain in Wales. Back in the Typewriter Age Rufus founded 'Pagans Against Nukes' - as a long time Pacifist he is interested in reclaiming the 'true' nature of those we have called 'War Goddesses'.

Alexis J. Money is a pagan artist, working on becoming a tattoo artist, and residing in the Northridge, CA area. She's happily married and lives with her husband, black cat, colored pencils, and assorted tattoo machines.

Copper Moon is a Morrigan devotee that shares her life with her cat Louis Maurice ('Moo'). Apart from her Morrigan time, she also enjoys reading and needlework.

Shea Morgan is the founder of Spirit's Edge (spiritsedge.org), its mystery school and spiritual community A Seeker's Salon. She is a Priestess of the Morrighan, Life Coach, Ordained Minister and teacher, inspiring seekers to find their own shining gems of Spirit within and to dream the life they were meant to live. She is a clairvoyant, clairaudient empath with a passion for shamanic healing, bringing the spiritual into manifestation in daily life through a partnership with the divine and allies in the plant, animal and mineral kingdoms. Shea is an Honored Member of the Temple of Witchcraft, graduate of the Temple's Mystery School and contributor to three Temple anthologies - *The Green Lovers: A Compilation of Plant Spirit Magic*, *The Waters and Fires of Avalon,* and *The Ancestors of the Craft*. She has studied with Martha Beck (Life Coach Training Program), the Foundation for Shamanic Studies and the don Miguel Ruiz family. She lives in St. Louis with her cats, and enjoys gardening, yoga, friends, family, and visiting the family "Century Farm," when she is not busy with her 25 year career in government affairs/public policy. Shea earned her MBA from the University of Missouri-St. Louis and her B.A. in Communications, Legal Institutions, Economics and Government from The American University in Washington, D.C.

Vivienne Moss spends her days brewing up trouble with her two daughters, and her nights casting spells. When she's not writing, you'll find her meandering through the enchanted forest with her witch sisters, her cat Marcee, and her dog Paco standing guard. A lover of all things occult, Vivienne dedicates her time to the study of esoteric knowledge. Vivienne's hope is to share the magic of the Other-Worlds with fellow seekers of Witchdom.

Sandy Nickell has opted not to provide a biography.

Morgaine Nightshade is a witch and priestess of The Morrigan, and a fantasy artist from Sweden. She is self-initiated and has been a follower of the Goddess for 10 years. Morgaine practices witchcraft, herbal medicine, meditation, and yoga.

Blackbird O'Connell is an Irish pagan (Págánacha) on the pagan path since 1999. She has dedicated herself to being a mother, an amateur author, a student, and an adviser as inspired by the ancient Druids. She serves the Tuatha Dé Danann by attempting to walk the Warrior path maintaining her life by the code of the Irish Fianna, "with Truth in her heart, strength in her arms, and fulfillment in her tongue."

Xochiquetzal Duti Odinsdottir is a pagan of the most eclectic sort. The work of blending the sacred and the profane makes for a most interesting journey. S/he counts the Morrighan as one of The Matrons and strives to honor the relationship. More about the work can be found at SacredProfanity.com.

Judith O'Grady is a Leaf on the God's Wind. She is an Irish Descendant and a Celt. One side of her family came from an island in the Far Wild West of Ireland and the other was mostly Welsh people who immigrated to hilly farm country in the New World and stayed there for hundreds of years. She describes this mixture as thinking with her dark Welsh head while feeling with her Black-Irish heart. When she was in her teens, she started researching her roots; reading folklore and history, anthropology and fiction. The Goddess to Whom she is dedicated pushed her to join in public ritual after thirty-odd years of worshipping alone and gradually this led to her being a member of the Ár nDraíocht Féin (ADF), completing their Dedicant's program, and being the Grove Organizer of the local Lake of Oaks Protogrove, ADF. With much less hesitancy, she started chatting on forums, blogging and spewing opinions in general, writing essays, poetry, and a small book.

 Among other things, **Kim Cairelle Perilloux** is a mixed-media Artist, a Writer, a Witch, a Gardener of herbs and flowers and weeds, and a delighted and often amused GiGi to her two sweet'um grandsons. She is the President and Executive Director of the New Orleans Black Hat Society and is Head Witch in Charge of its fundraiser gala, the New Orleans

Witches' Ball. Cairelle lives happily in her native New Orleans with her husband Kirk and their assortment of small furry bed hogs.

Monika Pleyer was born in November 1985 in a mountainous area in the middle of Germany, where old folk tales abound and spirits still roam free. This environment has shaped her so that from the time she could read, she's been devouring books on mythology, the afterlife, magic and the Gods and Goddesses of other cultures. When she's not writing poetry, you can always find her outside in thunderstorms, singing songs to her Gods and enjoying the rain.

Morpheus Ravenna is a spiritual worker, artist, teacher, and initiate of the Anderson Feri tradition of witchcraft, practicing the art for about twenty years. Her interests include folk magickal traditions, working with the land and natural forces, and Celtic heroic spirituality. She spearheads the Coru Cathubodua, a priesthood dedicated to the Morrigan. Her work at Stone City Pagan Sanctuary has helped provide a space for Pagan and nature-based community in northern California, and she recently appeared in the documentary "American Mystic." She can be reached through her website at beansidhe.net.

Sophie Reicher is a magician and devotional polytheist living in New York City. She is the author of "Spiritual Protection" and occasionally blogs at http://sreicher.weebly.com.

Juli D. Revezzo is a Florida girl with a love of fantasy, science fiction, and Arthurian legend, so much so she gained a B.A. in English and American Literature. She loves writing stories with fantastical elements whether it be a full-on fantasy, or a story set in this world–slightly askew. She has been published in short form in *Eternal Haunted Summer*, *Crossing the River: An Anthology In Honor of Sacred Journeys*, *Dark Things II: Cat Crimes* (a charity anthology for cat related charities), *Luna Station Quarterly*, *The Scribing Ibis: An Anthology of Pagan Fiction in Honor of Thoth*, and *Twisted Dreams Magazine*. She is author of *The Artist's Inheritance*, *Caitlin's Book of Shadows*, and *Drawing Down the Shades* (of the Antique Magic series) and has recently released her debut paranormal romance novel, *Passion's Sacred Dance*. She also has an article and book review or two out there. But her heart lies in the storytelling. She is a member of the Independent Author Network and the Magic Appreciation Tour. You can find out more about her at julidrevezzo.com

Michael Routery is a poet, writer, and educator. He is a Celtic reconstructionist polytheist and Druid, and a Hellenist as well. He is the author of *From the Prow of Myth*, a collection of devotional poetry from Vindos Press, and of numerous poems, stories, and essays, some of which can be found in various Bibliotheca Alexandrina anthologies, including *Written In Wine*, *Out of Arcadia*, *Unbound*, and *The Scribing Ibis*; more of his writing can be found in the Scarlet Imprint anthologies, *Datura* and *Mandragora*. He blogs at finnchuillsmast at wordpress.

David Salisbury is a queer, vegan, Witch and a devotee to the goddess Hekate. As High Priest of Coven of the Spiral Moon, he teaches Wicca and Witchcraft-based topics throughout the mid-Atlantic region. The focal point of his leadership is an activism and service-based approach that seeks to expand the unique gifts that each person came into the world with. He currently lives in Washington DC where he works to co-facilitate Firefly, a national Wiccan tradition.

Sarah Sinopa has been fascinated by the Morrigan since she was a little girl and was gifted with a small book of world Mythology. Out of all the stories within the story of the Morrigan was her favorite. Years later the Morrigan was still a persistent and ever present influence in her life. Sinopa honors Her still in art of all kinds.

L. Sixfingers first began writing about magick and witchery in junior high with her one-page newsletter, discreetly passed amongst students between classes. Since then she has continued to write and present her work at conferences and festivals. A feral creature of the Mórrígan, her work explores the intersections of identity, authenticity, devotional ecstasy, and (re)creating sustainable Pagan cultures. She is a Weaver (Priest/ess) of the Gathering Tradition, Witch, Pagan, and works full-time as a herbologist. In pursuit of enchantment, she lives in a traveling urban homestead with her love K. Heron and their lurcher pup Basil, creating mischief wherever she can, serving lots of tea, and dancing in communities ripe for revolution. Read more of her work at furioushorde.com and wortsandcunning.com. She can be contacted at travellingwitch@gmail.com.

Although not the original Diotima, **Diotima Sophia** does agree that the western world has invested far too much energy into separating the inseparable duo of mind and heart. Diotima has written widely on a number of subjects, including essays, fiction and poetry. Two of her latest books have been published by the Bibliotheca Alexandrina: *Dancing God* – a collection of poetry, and *Goat Foot God*, an examination of the Great God Pan; both are available through Neos Alexandria and can be found at neosalexandria.org/publishing.htm. Her latest work of fiction is *Tales in Vein*, a series of short stories available in ebook and audio book format from Amazon. Her website can be found at: diotima-sophia.com/.

Duane "**Raven Spirit**" Marshall is a 3rd degree Georgian (and Master Mason/Shriner) who has served as a regional coordinator for Kansas City Pagan Pride, as well as a Board

Member of International Pagan Pride. Currently he is HP of the Grove of the Old Ways in Kansas City, 2nd Lt Commander for his Legion of Honor (Shrine Vet club), President of his Clown Unit and Secretary for a Widows Sons Motorcycle club, as well as tyler for his Blue Lodge.

Sara Star is a traditional witch of the fairy faith who makes sacred art with homemade magical inks, paint and gold leaf. She lives in the Pacific Northwest with her family and her cat. Star's main influences are religious iconography, Frida Kahlo, and Gustav Klimt. More of her work can be found at etsy.com/shop/spiritscraft and spiritscraft.tumblr.com.

Stephanie Woodfield is the author of Celtic Lore and Spellcraft of the Dark Goddess: Invoking the Morrigan. Stephanie has been a practicing Witch and Priestess of the Morrigan for over sixteen years. Her articles have appeared in SageWoman magazine and on the Witches Voice website. She is one of the founding members of Morrigu's Daughters, an online sisterhood dedicated to the Morrigan. You can her on her blog Dark Goddess Musings darkgoddessmusings.blogspot.com/.

About Bibliotheca Alexandrina

Ptolemy Soter, the first Makedonian ruler of Egypt, established the library at Alexandria to collect all of the world's learning in a single place. His scholars compiled definitive editions of the Classics, translated important foreign texts into Greek, and made monumental strides in science, mathematics, philosophy and literature. By some accounts over a million scrolls were housed in the famed library, and though it has long since perished due to the ravages of war, fire, and human ignorance, the image of this great institution has remained as a powerful inspiration down through the centuries.

To help promote the revival of traditional polytheistic religions we have launched a series of books dedicated to the ancient gods of Greece and Egypt. The library is a collaborative effort drawing on the combined resources of the different elements within the modern Hellenic and Kemetic communities, in the hope that we can come together to praise our gods and share our diverse understandings, experiences and approaches to the divine.

A list of our current and forthcoming titles can be found on the following page. For more information on the Bibliotheca, our submission requirements for upcoming devotionals, or to learn about our organization, please visit us at neosalexandria.org.

Sincerely,

The Editorial Board of the Library of Neos Alexandria

Current Titles

Written in Wine: A Devotional Anthology for Dionysos
Dancing God: Poetry of Myths and Magicks
Goat Foot God
Longing for Wisdom: The Message of the Maxims
The Phillupic Hymns
Unbound: A Devotional Anthology for Artemis
Waters of Life: A Devotional Anthology for Isis and Serapis
Bearing Torches: A Devotional Anthology for Hekate
Queen of the Great Below: An Anthology in Honor of Ereshkigal
From Cave to Sky: A Devotional Anthology in Honor of Zeus
Out of Arcadia: A Devotional Anthology for Pan
Anointed: A Devotional Anthology for the Deities
    of the Near and Middle East
The Scribing Ibis: An Anthology of Pagan Fiction in Honor of Thoth
Queen of the Sacred Way: A Devotional Anthology
    in Honor of Persephone
Unto Herself: A Devotional Anthology for Independent Goddesses
The Shining Cities: An Anthology of Pagan Science Fiction
Guardian of the Road: A Devotional Anthology in Honor of Hermes
Harnessing Fire: A Devotional Anthology in Honor of Hephaestus
Beyond the Pillars: An Anthology of Pagan Fantasy
Queen of Olympos: A Devotional Anthology for Hera and Iuno
A Mantle of Stars: A Devotional Anthology
    in Honor of the Queen of Heaven
Crossing the River: An Anthology in Honor of Sacred Journeys

Forthcoming Titles

Potnia: An Anthology in Honor of Demeter
The Queen of the Sky Who Rules Over All the Gods:
    A Devotional Anthology in Honor of Bast
Daughter of the Sun: A Devotional Anthology in Honor of Sekhmet
Seasons of Grace: A Devotional in Honor of the Muses,
    the Charites, and the Horae
From the Roaring Deep: A Devotional for Poseidon
    and the Spirits of the Sea
Shield of Wisdom: A Devotional Anthology in Honor of Athena
Megaloi Theoi: A Devotional Anthology for the Dioskouroi
    and Their Families
Sirius Rising: A Devotional Anthology for Cynocephalic Deities

CPSIA information can be obtained
at www.ICGtesting.com
Printed in the USA
LVOW04s2209230316
480503LV00028B/587/P

9 781500 566562